Stress That Motivates

Self-Talk Secrets for Success

Revised Edition

Dru Scott, Ph.D.

:50™

A FIFTY-MINUTE™ SERIES BOOK

Viva Books Private Limited

New Delhi • Mumbai • Chennai • Kolkata • Bangalore • Hyderabad

First Indian Edition 2004
Reprinted 2005

VIVA BOOKS PRIVATE LIMITED

- 4262/3 Ansari Road, Daryaganj, New Delhi 110 002
  E-mail: viva@vivagroupindia.net
- 215-216 New Apollo Estate, 2nd Floor, Mogra Lane, Andheri (E),
  Mumbai 400 069 E-mail: vivamumbai@vivagroupindia.net
- Jamals Fazal Chambers, 26 Greams Road, Chennai 600 006
  E-mail: vivachennai@vivagroupindia.net
- B-103, Jindal Towers, 21/1A/3 Darga Road, Kolkata 700 017
  E-mail: vivakolkata@vivagroupindia.net
- 7 GF, Sovereign Park Apts., 56-58 K.R. Road, Basavanagudi,
  Bangalore 560 004 E-mail: vivabangalore@vivagroupindia.net
- 101 & 102, First Floor, Mughal Marg Apartments, Narayanaguda,
  Hyderabad 500 029 E-mail: vivahyderabad@vivagroupindia.net

Published by arrangement with

Crisp Publications, Inc.
1200 Hamilton Court,
Menlo Park
CA 94025
USA

Credits:
Senior Editor: Debbie Woodbury
Editor: Ann Gosch
Assistant Editor: Genevieve Del Rosario
Production Managers: Judy Petry
Design: Nicole Phillips
Production Artist: Zach Hooker

ISBN 81-7649-709-6

Published by Vinod Vasishtha for Viva Books Private Limited, 4262/3 Ansari Road, Daryaganj, New Delhi 110 002 and printed & bound at Raj Press, R-3 Inderpuri, New Delhi-110 012

Learning Objectives For:

STRESS THAT MOTIVATES

The objectives for *Stress That Motivates* are listed below. They have been developed to guide you, the reader, to the core issues covered in this book.

THE OBJECTIVES OF THIS BOOK ARE:

- ❑ 1) To show the powerful link between stress, motivation, and self-talk
- ❑ 2) To give you tools for self-protection and self-motivation in stressful situations
- ❑ 3) To expose the five biggest traps in self-talk
- ❑ 4) To give you a ready-to-use reinforcement system that will help you cut stress, build motivation, and get the right things done

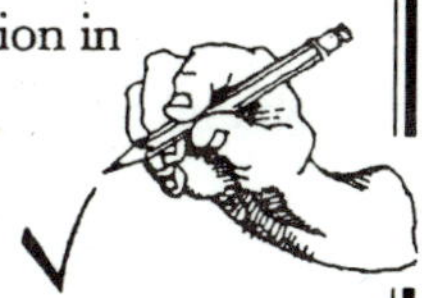

ASSESSING YOUR PROGRESS

In addition to the learning objectives, Crisp Learning has developed an **assessment** that covers the fundamental information presented in this book. A 25-item, multiple-choice and true-false questionnaire allows the reader to evaluate his or her comprehension of the subject matter. To learn how to obtain a copy of this assessment, please call **1-800-442-7477** and ask to speak with a Customer Service Representative.

Assessments should not be used in any employee selection process.

Congratulations

The fact that you are reading this book tells you one of two things:

- If someone gave you this book, it shows that someone believes in you and wants you to get even more from life.
- If you bought this book for yourself, it shows that you are not content with the status quo. You want continuous improvement for yourself and your organization.

In either case, you are moving ahead with each line you read and with each exercise you explore. You are taking positive steps toward enriching your life–on the job and at home.

About the Author

Dru Scott is an internationally known author and seminar speaker. Her five books and six films are used around the world. Many of the principles in this book were researched and funded as part of her work with DuPont.

How to Use This Book

This *Fifty-Minute*™ *Series Book* is a unique, user-friendly product. As you read through the material, you will quickly experience the interactive nature of the book. There are numerous exercises, real-world case studies, and examples that invite your opinion, as well as checklists, tips, and concise summaries that reinforce your understanding of the concepts presented.

A Crisp Learning *Fifty-Minute*™ *Book* can be used in a variety of ways. Individual self-study is one of the most common. However, many organizations use *Fifty-Minute* books for pre-study before a classroom training session. Other organizations use the books as a part of a systemwide learning program–supported by video and other media based on the content in the books. Still others work with Crisp Learning to customize the material to meet their specific needs and reflect their culture. Regardless of how it is used, we hope you will join the more than 20 million satisfied learners worldwide who have completed a *Fifty-Minute Book.*

Preface

As I've talked with friends and customers over the years, they've often asked me, "When are you going to write a book on that motivation system you teach?" With a sense of excitement, I can give a resounding, "Now!"

This system generates a special passion for me because it has helped so many people cut stress, add energy, and get the right things done. This system does work, and it is fun, interesting, and practical.

But my biggest challenge in using the system arrived when–after being single most of my life–I married a widower and became a stepmother to three teenagers. I learned the meaning of stress in a new way. A friend had told me that marriage is God's cure for rigidity and self-centeredness. She was right. At the beginning, I was convinced that my new family needed to make all the improvements. But I learned that my own to-do list needed to include making improvements–particularly in my attitude. I had used this self-talk system for work stresses and accomplishments, and I now also use it in my personal life. And so do thousands of people.

This revision includes the feedback from so many people who used the first edition. It also shows the personal benefits of the system more clearly. And it contains a ready-to-use set of Quick-Start Reinforcements.

Whether the stresses and changes you are facing are in your personal life or at work, this simple system will help you. It's easy. It's practical. It takes only a few minutes a day. And it will help you gain relief, build your energy, and get the right things done.

Dru Scott

Dru Scott, Ph.D.
San Francisco

Contents

Part 5: Procrastination and Motivation: Four Great Techniques

Part 6: Mega Motivation with Pictures of Excellence

Part 7: Reinforcements that Work

Part 8: Persistence, Pictures, and a Happy Ending

Part 9: The Seven-Day Quick Start

P A R T 1

The Big Connection Between Stress, Motivation, and Self-Talk

"*While we cannot direct the wind, we can adjust the sails.*"

–Author unknown

SUCCESS SECRET

Most people have never been told how big the connection is between stress, motivation, and self-talk.

Putting the Big Connection to Work for You

You can walk into almost any group, ask people to raise their hands if they are feeling stress today, and see hands fly up across the room. You can also ask that same group to raise their hands if they have received any training on how change and stress interrelate, and you will see hands staying down. And when you ask if they have received any instruction on how stress is increased or decreased by what they say to themselves, you will see those hands staying down again.

Few people have been given an easy way to build a bridge from stress and negative results of change to motivation and effectiveness.

Helping Three Groups of People

That's why the three groups below welcome the system in *Stress That Motivates* so enthusiastically. You may identify with more than one of these groups:

- People who feel stress and want relief and recovery
- People who face changes and want survival and success
- People who carry responsibilities and want to be up, energetic, and productive *consistently*

The ideas in this book are not dry, dead, academic research. They are lively, practical ideas for handling stress. Plus, they include a quick and powerful system to help you know what to do *and* how to do it consistently.

In this part, you'll find answers to:

- What are the most important ideas in this book and how can they assist me?
- What are the major causes of stress?
- What are five tools I can take away from this part?

To introduce you to the dramatic improvements possible with the *Stress That Motivates* system, let's look at the lives of two people who each faced a mountain of stress.

Two Stories to Inspire You

Here is an introduction to Barbara and Doug, their stresses, and the improvements they gained. This introduction gives you an encouraging glimpse of the overall life improvements possible. Their full stories are revealed later in this book.

The Beginning of the Barbara Story

Two years ago, Barbara was 70 pounds overweight. She told people that her boss didn't like anything she did, and she told herself that she had too much stress. She also told herself that she had every reason to feel stress. She had gone through a divorce from an alcoholic husband, lost her house, and been forced to pack her son and daughter and their belongings into her car and move in with her mother.

Then Barbara found a way to face her situation and turn her stress into motivation.

Today, Barbara stood up, smiled, straightened her size-6 red jacket, and walked to the front of the conference room. She smiled even more widely as her boss announced that the envelope being put in her hands contained an accomplishment award of $1,000.

The next story introduces a different stress turnaround.

The Beginning of the Doug Story

A year and half ago, Doug pulled into his garage at 6:30 Friday night and announced to his waiting wife, "I'm sick of it all. I'm tired of the idiots on the freeway. I'm tired of the warehouse that's so screwed up I have to drive miles across town to make an emergency delivery. The job's impossible. My new boss is impossible–a total turkey. And I just found out that I have to meet with him again on Monday because I've missed a few quotas."

Then Doug found a way to face his situation and turn his stress into motivation.

One Friday six months later, Doug pulled his car into his driveway as he whistled along with his favorite CD.

He smiled and puffed out his chest because he had planned his territory and calls so effectively and worked so well with the warehouse that he met quota for weekly sales early on Friday.

He told himself, "Good going!" because he was home at 3:00 this Friday. As he stepped out of the car, he smiled again as he reached for the two tickets in his coat pocket that he and his wife were going to use that night.

You will learn more about Doug and Barbara later in the book, and you'll find out what else they faced and what they did.

Practical and Positive Ideas

Even though your situation may be different from Barbara's or Doug's, as you read the rest of their stories and those of others in this book, you will find practical and positive ideas for turning stress into motivation even in the face of big problems, changes, and demands.

To give you a head start, let's look at an overview of the book on the next page.

Book Overview

The purpose of this book is simple. It is to encourage you to read and use the last chapter. But please don't turn there now because over the years of helping thousands of people use this *Stress That Motivates* system, I've discovered something. The people who use the method to change their lives are the people who have taken time to understand the secrets and the stories behind the system. (If, however, your curiosity is bubbling over, you can take a peek and come back.)

If a change or a demand confronts us and
we deny it or do nothing,
we have stress that damages.

But when we respond to a change or a demand
by accepting our current reality and
by taking purposeful action,
we have stress that motivates.

This *purposeful action for improvement* can be toward
a total solution (your picture of excellence),
a partial solution, or
the mastery of containment.

Even if our action does not totally solve the situation,
it helps us feel better and work better.

The secret to training ourselves to take this action
consistently is *positive and purposeful self-talk.*

The Strategy—Mental Background Music

You may be asking, "How could such a simple system of purposeful and positive self-talk bring about such big improvements?" Here's how.

Simply defined, self-talk is what we repeat to ourselves–our mental background music. Most of us are not even conscious of our self-talk, yet it has a powerful influence on our stress, motivation, and actions.

What you tell yourself over and over either helps you or hinders you. It either triggers stress or encourages moving ahead. It sets your mood. It helps you feel tired or energetic. It turns the tap for stagnation or creativity. It prompts inaction or action. You will see a powerful experiment that proves this point when you come to the section on "The Downers and Drainers" and "The Leaders and Lifters."

The quickest way for people to train themselves to use this action approach consistently is to reinforce themselves with positive, purposeful self-talk. The right reinforcements encourage the right actions.

We are talking to ourselves all the time, so why not make all our self-talk–our mental background music–encouraging, enjoyable, and effective?

What If Your Situation Is Different?

Some people might be thinking,

"But what if you don't totally control the situation."

Many people rightfully make this comment. They do face situations that they do not totally control. This means it is twice as important to focus on what they can control. And with the right method, they can control what they say to themselves even in times of stress.

Others might object,

"But I don't have time."

Here's the good part. In this book, you will learn how to turn a few minutes in the morning and evening into a daily tune-up that gives you surprising benefits throughout the day. It is like the man playing a guitar that is not tuned. He can play it faster or harder, but it won't help. He needs to tune it so he can play the music that is within him.

During these morning and evening minutes, you give your background music a tune-up. You prepare your mind for the right action–particularly in times of stress.

The Major Cause of Stress

Pioneer stress researcher Hans Selye, M.D., defines stress as "the non-specific response of the body to any demand made upon it." This classic definition given in *Stress with Distress* spotlights change and the demands it makes on people to adapt. Because change is closely linked with stress, consider what often happens. Changes, demands, and stress often arrive at the door at the same time. Yet, we rarely ask why this is.

Stress and Ignoring Changes

Dr. Selye is right. A major cause of stress is this: changes that are ignored. When a change arrives on our doorstep and we do nothing about it, stress is likely.

This is not the same as only thinking positively about a situation, as you'll see in this case.

Peter's Story

Peter leaned across his executive desk and commented, "I don't see why people talk about stress so much. There is so much discussion about stress. When I walk out on the plant floor or sit down and talk to one of our employees, I always hear about *stress.*

"I don't know about stress, but I do know something I've told myself for years: When I run into a tough situation, I dig into the problem, I find out what needs to be done, and *I do something about it.*"

Indeed, Peter does have the answer in three steps:

Face it. Understand it. And do something about it.

As Peter said, "When I run into a tough situation, I analyze the problem, I see what needs to be done, and *I do something about it.*" This means facing the change, understanding the change, seeing what needs to be done, and then doing something about it.

Changes that are ignored and purposeful action not taken rank as major causes of stress, but another cause is beliefs that don't work.

The Impact of Belief System on Stress

Our belief system shapes more of our lives than most of us have been taught. We may not be able to change the entire situation, but we can change our belief systems, according to Paul D. Ware, M.D., who was named the Outstanding Teacher of Behavioral Medicine in the United States. Having trained psychiatrists and psychologists for 30 years, he now heads two psychiatric hospitals in Shreveport, Louisiana, and reports:

Few people are told how much impact what they say to themselves has on how much stress they feel. What people say to themselves about an experience–their self-talk–often has more impact on their lives than the experience itself.

Most stress is not caused by external circumstances. It is caused by our belief systems.

Our choices and the way we perceive and react to life experiences cause the bulk of our stress. So much of stress has to do with people's belief systems. And we can change our belief systems.

The person who learned early in life to think "I can solve problems" or "I can figure things out" has less stress than most people. The person who did not learn this belief as a child can learn it as an adult.

When people are feeling stress, they need to hear healing beliefs over and over.

When Dr. Ware deals with people undergoing stress, he encourages them to remember: You can take care of yourself. You can stay aware of your own needs and wants and take care of them in positive ways. You can get information and make good decisions. You know more about you than anyone else. You have solved problems in the past, and you can solve them now.

Our belief systems do influence our stress–and our motivations.

Stress and Beliefs About Difficulty

Some people believe that any situation that is difficult deserves the label of stress. Yet think of how many people do difficult things and smile as they tell about it. Running a marathon. Building a summer cabin. Hiking a mountain. Completing a class. Passing an exam. All these are difficult, but they are rarely described as stressful, for one reason: The purpose and direction are clear.

When you talk further about stress, something else surfaces–confusion and chaos. That's what deserves the stress label. Consider the stress in not knowing what to do next, having no clear purpose, inconsistent rules, changing directions, no milestones, no finish line. That's confusion and that's stress.

Beliefs About Motivation

Some people believe motivation is happiness. They picture Snoopy in the Peanuts cartoon, the dog with the big smile, the spinning ears, and the dancing feet who stays in one place. But motivation is more than happiness and enthusiasm.

Motivation is the quality of having a motive or incentive that *stirs us to action.* This motive for action moves us toward our dreams and objectives. The motivated person's feet do not stay in one place. They move forward to a desired outcome. A picture of motivation is the runner who is looking forward and pressing toward the goal.

Motivation draws us toward our objectives. Stress hinders us from knowing and moving toward our objectives–unless we train ourselves with self-talk reinforcements to respond consistently with purposeful action.

Now that you know the big ideas in the book and two big causes of stress, here are five tools for self-motivation in stressful situations.

Tool 1: A Checklist for Your Priorities

The list below may include some issues you are currently grappling with. You will want to refer to this list later, so take a few moments now and check (✔) the issues you currently face in your personal and professional life:

- ❑ Reducing stress
- ❑ Building motivation
- ❑ Catching up
- ❑ Handling negative people
- ❑ Taming procrastination
- ❑ Communicating a picture of where you want to go
- ❑ Learning new skills
- ❑ Keeping up an energetic attitude
- ❑ Taking care of your own needs and wants in constructive ways
- ❑ Dealing with rejection
- ❑ Getting organized
- ❑ Learning new habits
- ❑ Listening more effectively
- ❑ Breaking bad habits
- ❑ Gaining more self-discipline
- ❑ Learning new skills more rapidly
- ❑ Implementing plans more effectively

Keep your selections in mind as you explore this book. Let your checked items be a mental magnet, drawing your thinking to practical ideas that will help you achieve what you want.

The exercise on the next page gives you a chance to probe into on-the-job and personal situations you want to improve.

Tool 2: A Diagram to Speed the Improvements You Want

The diagram below will help you visualize the role of self-talk in determining your motivation and stress levels. This flow chart depicts how we experience external events and distill them into internal feelings of stress or motivation.

The Big Connection: Stress, Motivation, and Self-Talk

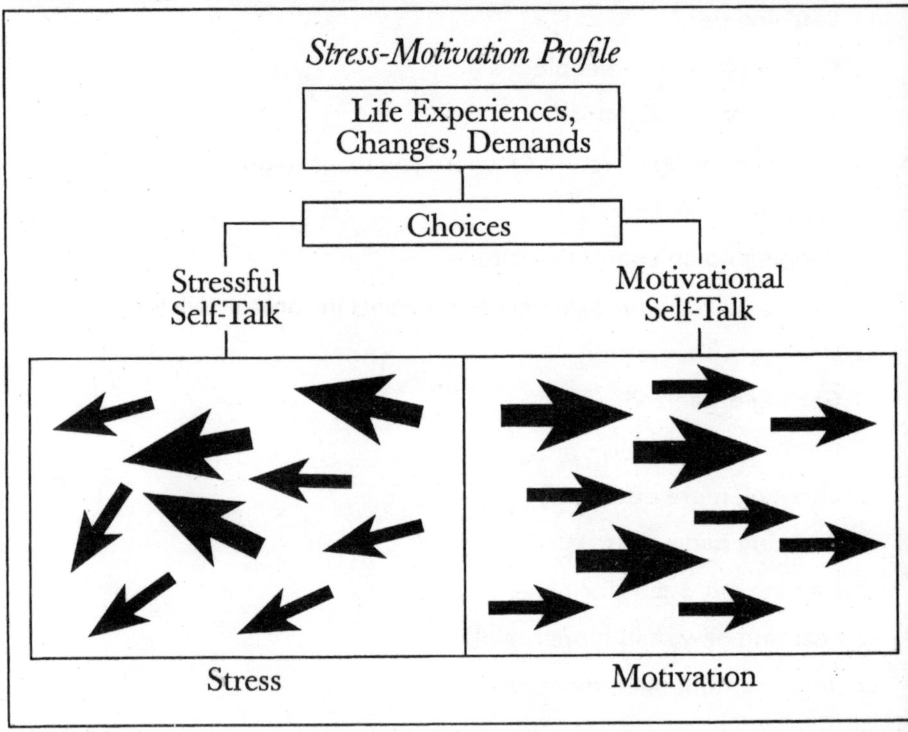

At the top of the chart are life experiences–those events, good or bad, pleasant or unpleasant–that we all encounter. We process these experiences by making choices. Psychiatrist Frank Minirth, co-founder of the Minirth–Meier Clinic, says "Choices are the hinges of destiny." The point of choice is where our pathway branches either toward greater stress or greater motivation. The determining factor is the self-talk we choose. We can describe any life experience as a disaster or a challenge, an intrusion or an opportunity, a roadblock or a problem to be solved. We can say either, "there is nothing I can do" or "there is always something I can do."

For Faster Improvements

You enjoy faster and greater improvements in life when you live by these life-changing realities:

- We have the power to choose how we define every life experience.
- The way we define our life experiences is revealed in how we talk to ourselves about those experiences.
- Some self-talk leads to stress–drained energy, chaotic thinking, indecision, lack of resolution.
- Other self-talk leads to motivation–incentive, direction, purpose, problem solving, problem prevention, and positive action toward achieving desired results and dreams.

Though people cannot control every life experience, they can control what they say to themselves about the experience.

According to Dr. Ware, few people are told how much impact their self-talk–what they say to themselves–has on how much stress they feel. What people say to themselves about an experience, he says, often has more impact on their lives than the experience itself.

Tool 3: A Quote List that Sounds the Stress-Warning Buzzer

As you read this section, you may experience an inner tug. You may feel one or more of the following responses bubbling up into your mind about your situation:

> *"My situation is different."*
>
> *"There's nothing I can do."*
>
> *"It will never work."*
>
> *"I don't have time."*
>
> *"I tried it once, and it didn't work."*
>
> *"It's not that easy."*
>
> *"There is too much to do."*
>
> *"You don't know the people I work with."*
>
> *"It doesn't feel natural."*
>
> *"I know this already."*

In the next part, we will look closely at these responses. Meanwhile, do not be concerned if you identify with some of these statements. Many people do at first. Do not be surprised if, by the time you finish reading this book, doing the exercises, and putting the principles into practice, you feel the best ever with new spirit and attitude.

When you think about spirit and attitude, the next idea is a good one to keep at hand.

Tool 4: A Story to Stimulate *Your* Success

Charles Fletcher Lummis, author and crusader for Indian rights, once said, "I am bigger than anything that can happen to me. All these things–sorrow, misfortune, and suffering–are outside my door. I am in the house and I have the key." The key Lummis is talking about is choice–the ability to choose our own self-talk.

Larry's Story

The amazing power that lies in our ability to choose is vividly demonstrated in the story of Larry, who underwent a life experience more shattering and painful than anything most people will ever have to endure. He survived that experience because, as Lummis put it, he chose to view misfortune and suffering as "outside his door."

Larry, a top-producing financial consultant, sat at a luncheon table after a seminar. The people at his table, whom he had just met, were painfully polite, going to near-ridiculous extremes to pretend they did not notice the scars on Larry's face and hands. Larry was familiar with other people's uneasiness, and he was a master in telling his story and encouraging people to feel relaxed.

"In case you're wondering about these scars," he said, "I don't mind talking about it. A few years ago, I survived a fiery plane crash."

"It must have been awful," someone ventured.

"Awful? Yes," Larry replied. "But when I got out of the plane, the first thing I thought was, 'I'm still alive!' They took me to the hospital, where I underwent the first surgery to reconstruct my face and arms. Altogether I went through 74 operations–nine on my hands alone. What got me through it all was a choice I made. I decided to say to myself, 'This is just a temporary inconvenience.' Talking about that entire experience as a 'temporary inconvenience' made it bearable. Anything that has happened to me since then is microscopic in comparison."

Larry's life is an inspiring story and a memorable way to bring this part to a close. His courage shows so clearly the power of our choices.

Wrap-Up for Part 1

To implant these truths in your mind and fortify your power to recall, check (✔) the ideas that are the most important to you:

- ❑ While I cannot control every event in life, I can control what I say to myself about the experience.
- ❑ I have the power to choose how I define any life experience.
- ❑ The way I define a life experience is revealed in how I talk to myself about the experience.
- ❑ Some self-talk leads to stress.
- ❑ Other self-talk leads to motivation.
- ❑ What I say to myself frequently has more impact on my life than the actual experience.
- ❑ The stress that motivates is the stress I respond to by taking action toward a solution or toward containment and mastery.
- ❑ The most powerful way to train myself to take this action is with systematic and purposeful self-talk.

In the next part, you will learn what your parents, teachers, and employers may never have told you about stress and motivation.

PART 2

What They Didn't Tell You About Stress and Motivation

> *"Many persons have a wrong idea of what constitutes true happiness. It is not attained through self-gratification but through fidelity to a worthy purpose."*
>
> –Helen Keller

SUCCESS SECRET

Knowledge is power.

Because rapid change increases both stress factors and the need for motivation, it pays to keep up-to-date on the dynamics of both.

The Accumulation of Stress

Harry leaned forward with both hands chopping through the air to emphasize his excitement. "Man, oh, man!" he exclaimed. "I wish I'd heard all this a few years ago. I didn't know what was happening to me! When I heard 'stress,' I thought it meant just being fed up. But I was going through honest-to-goodness stress and burnout and didn't even know it!"

Harry's face and eyes lit up. There was almost a light bulb shining over his head as he continued. "There I was, eating all the time–not hungry, just grazing. I had trouble sleeping, trouble concentrating. I was getting so forgetful I thought I had Alzheimer's disease.

"I finally went to the doctor. The doc examined me and asked a lot of questions. I told her about my new job, about moving to a new city, and putting on 20 pounds. Our daughter and her baby have moved in with us for who knows how long. After the exam the doc assured me that my problems were stress-related. Now that I understand the whole stress thing better, it's obvious. But it wasn't then."

Get a Medical Checkup

Take a lesson from Harry. If you are feeling a lot of stress, see your physician. There may be physiological causes of stress in addition to the psychological issues covered in this book. If you are interested in the medical aspects of stress, also see the comprehensive article, "The Concepts of Stress and Stress System Disorders," in the *Journal of the American Medical Association.*

Knowledge about Stress and Motivation is Power

In this part we will delve into truths about stress that many people have never been told. Like Harry, you may see a light turn on as you connect these truths with your experience. Once you have an understanding of what stress is and how it affects you, you will have the power to manage it, direct it, and use it as a motivating force.

After reading this part, you will be better equipped to:

- ➤ Spot early warning signals of trouble ahead
- ➤ Add more lift to your life with strong motivational ingredients

Stress Factors

Things that drain and drag on us, that pull and tug, can mount up, particularly in times of change. Most of us are not consciously aware of how much stress we are under or what we can do about it. But there are simple, revealing insights and exercises to uncover these stress factors. The following will help you *turn on the light* and see how to handle stress even more effectively.

Insight 1:
You Can Predict When You Are Most Likely to Feel Stressed

Pay special attention when:

- You feel overwhelmed or flooded
- The stress is too intense
- The duration is too long
- The end is not in sight

In addition to the actual experience, consider how statements you make also can cause feelings of stress to skyrocket:

"I just can't cope."

"It will never end."

"There is nothing I can do."

"I just can't handle it."

"This is too much."

These statements handcuff a person's ability to think clearly and creatively when that ability is most needed. You can also predict stress when you *feel*:

- You are alone
- No one is there for you
- You are not appreciated

Feelings magnify stress. Some people may have an extensive support group within arms' reach, yet still *feel* alone. Others may *feel* unappreciated even when people appreciate them. On the other hand, people feel differently when they say to themselves:

"I find the right people at the right time."

"I take care of my own needs and wants, and I do it without hurting myself or others."

"I appreciate myself and what I do."

Insight 2:
Calling a Short Timeout Helps Reduce Stress

Dr. Ware recommends this quick timeout. People who train themselves to use this surprisingly powerful four-step tool can get themselves right back on track. Say and implement the following:

If I am feeling overwhelmed, I protect myself by taking time out for a few minutes so I can think clearly and creatively.

1. I relax and breathe deeply.
2. I accept my feelings and the realities of my current situation.
3. I picture in my imagination how I want the situation to be.
4. I take action to get there. I do something purposeful even if it is not the total solution. I work toward a solution or mastery of the situation.

Please see the quick and easy way to remember the four steps on the next page.

A Baseball Memory Hook for a Quick Timeout

An easy way to remember the four timeout steps is to picture a baseball diamond with one step at each base.

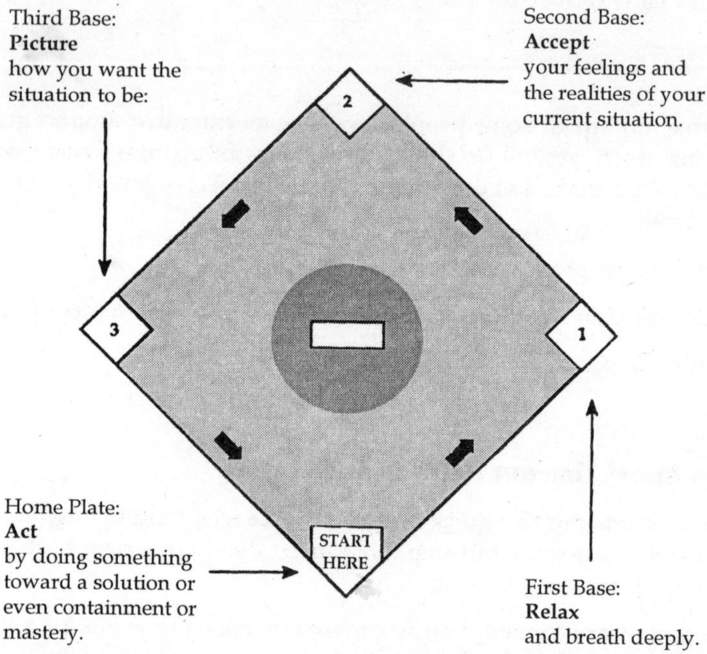

People who feel considerable stress may spend a few minutes in this timeout three or four times a day. One man said he stares intently at a printout on his desk and mentally works through the four bases. "The results," he said, "are so much better than telling myself, 'I can't cope. I'll never get caught up,' and then feeling frozen for an hour."

Remember the baseball diamond with RAPiD. R for *relax*; A for *accept*; P for *picture*; and D for *do something*.

Practice

Because this short timeout has so much value for keeping stress in its place, take a moment now. Write the ideas on a card or in a handy place. Have them available for when you feel stress coming.

Insight 3:
You Can Predict Stressful Burnout from Eight General Signals

The terms stress and burnout are often used interchangeably. The eight general signals of burnout are listed below. See if you find yourself or people you know described in this list.

1. Communicating less.

A person with this signal might say less at meetings. He might feel dismayed whenever the phone rings. Rather than talking with his family at breakfast, he reads the cereal box.

2. Feeling less energy.

This shows up in different ways. The most common description is feeling as though a person's gears are turning, but there is sawdust slowing down the gears.

3. Experiencing lower productivity.

The person with lower productivity usually notices it long before anyone else. She might go home at night and ask herself, "What did I accomplish today?" She is hard-pressed for a good answer.

4. Arriving late more often for work or appointments.

It is logical that less energy would lead to being late more often.

5. Experiencing sleep disturbance.

Sleep disturbance takes different forms. The person may have trouble going to sleep and then wake up in the middle of the night–usually around 3 A.M.–and not be able to go back to sleep. Or the person may want to sleep all the time. Those with this form of sleep disturbance might turn on the television and drift into sleep long before the end of a program.

6. Experiencing appetite disturbance.

Unplanned weight loss is the most common signal, but appetite disturbance can exhibit itself as unplanned weight gain. Such a person may want to eat all the time. Tip-offs include after-dinner grazing, looking into the refrigerator, and rummaging through the cupboards. The person eats even when there is no physical hunger.

7. Feeling preoccupied with health and body.

It is good to be conscientious about exercise and good eating, but people experiencing stress and burnout often become highly focused on their physical selves. They think and talk about their bodily functions and sensations much of the time.

8. Having decreased wants.

The person loses interest in the world. Picture an interviewer handing out a lined pad with this request: Write down everything you want to do, re-do, read, write, reorganize, discuss, see, hear, visit, clean out, catch up, or buy.

People with little stress or who are managing stress well will take the pad, and the pen will fly. They will fill up four or five pages without letup and still have plenty of ideas.

People who feel stressed and burned out are another picture. They will stare at the pad, write a few lines, sigh, and put down the pen.

Practice

With which of these signals do you identify?

____

____

Insight 4:
You Can Spot Burnout from Three Specific Signals

In addition to the eight general signals of burnout, individuals also might exhibit one or more of three specific telltale signals:

1. Experiencing decreased concentration.

A person might become very susceptible to interruptions, from others as well as from oneself. Standing by a file drawer, the person knows he walked over to get something; but after putting his hand on the drawer, he wonders, Now, what was I looking for?

2. Feeling suspicious of other people's joy.

Imagine a person who is feeling burned out about life in general. If she sees people whistling as they work and tackling tough jobs with gusto, the burned-out person may narrow her eyes, scowl at the upbeat people, and mutter, "Those hypocrites! They can't really feel like that."

3. Taking things personally.

People experiencing burnout often become self-focused. They question events with, "Why did this happen to *me*? Why did he say that to *me*?" During burnout, empathy for others is on the back burner.

For example, a person walks down the office hallway. Approaching from the other direction is a manager from another division–a nodding acquaintance, hardly a close friend. While passing in the hall, the manager seems hurried, does not say hello, and does not even make eye contact. A person who is managing stress well would attach no importance to the incident. At most, such a person would assume the manager was distracted or in a hurry. But a burned-out person might begin to worry, "Why is the manager mad at *me*?"

Practice

What are your specific signals?

____

____

Insight 5:
Burnout Is Stressful and Common but Not Mandatory

Do not feel cheated if you are not feeling burned out. Even though someone says that everybody in your job gets burned out, do not believe it.

Insight 6:
Language Can Alert You to Stress

A recent informal study conducted in a major American corporation showed convincingly that language is an important indicator of stress. The study was conducted over a seven-year period and involved interviews with more than 4,000 people in everyday work situations. Researchers studied verbatim transcripts of these interviews.

People who described themselves as under stress tended to use certain kinds of statements more than three times more often than other individuals. The results were consistent. A clear link between stress and stressful language was established.

Ten of the most common stressful statements were listed in Part 1, and they are repeated below. Read through the statements and check (✔) any that you recall saying a number of times in the last week.

- ❑ My situation is different.
- ❑ There's nothing I can do.
- ❑ It will never work.
- ❑ I don't have time.
- ❑ There's too much to do.
- ❑ I tried it once and it didn't work.
- ❑ It's not that easy.
- ❑ You don't know the people I work with
- ❑ It doesn't feel natural.
- ❑ I know this already.

Practice

When you think about yourself and these statements, how would you rate yourself on a scale of 1 to 10? (1 = Feeling a lot of stress–The road is bumpy. 10 = Feeling no stress–It's a smooth, clear road ahead.)

What changes might you make after looking at the list of stressful language? Th list shows the intimate link between stress and the language of self-talk. Think how much impact language has on beliefs and behavior–especially when we repeat messages to ourselves again and again.

Insight 7:
Exercise Is the Best Way to Reduce Stressful Burnout

Getting a good supply of oxygen to your brain still tops the list of ways to reduce stress. The reason is that oxygen helps you think clearly and creatively. Yet exercise is the last thing most people feel like doing when they feel stress.

The good news is that to make a difference, you need not run a marathon. The exercise that provides the best benefit with the least risk is walking. Walking only two miles a day is so important that many therapists recommend it as a prerequisite for starting treatment for severe burnout. Whether it is walking or another form of exercise, carve out time for yourself.

Taking care of yourself in positive ways such as exercise helps you be your best for everyone in your life.

Insight 8:
Taking Care of Yourself in Positive Ways Lessens Stress

This is obvious. When you satisfy your own needs and wants in constructive ways, you have more energy to take action. You avoid the temptation that often goes along with stress–feeling that other people should be doing more for you. You have an easier time tackling the responsibilities you face. When you keep your psychological tank on full, everyone benefits. You are a much better person to be around. You can serve others much more effectively.

Keeping Your Tank Full

Considering how well you are keeping yourself filled with psychological satisfaction, where would your gauge be?

E 1/2 F

As one woman laughingly related, "I used to think the line was, Love your neighbor *instead* of yourself. The real message is, Love your neighbor *as* yourself." Take care of yourself. Do it in ways that do not hurt yourself, others, or your situation.

Motivation—A Strong Sense of Direction Cuts the Stress

You rarely read in the popular press about the importance of purpose and direction in reducing stress. Yet a sense of purpose and direction in our lives–a sense of motivation–is the key to managing and conquering stress.

The word motivation comes from the Latin *movere*, which means to *move*. Motivation suggests energy, drive, persistence, accomplishments, teamwork, satisfaction. These are things we all want, things every organization wants. Yet we often overlook the core meaning of motivation.

Motivation Means Motive

Motivation means having a strong inner incentive to action–action toward a goal, action with a purpose. Consequently, being motivated means knowing where you want to go. It means knowing your dreams, objectives, and chosen destination.

The following will help you gain a stronger sense of your own motives and motivation factors.

Are You Ready to Win Big?

For each of the following exercises, rate yourself on a scale of 1 to 10.

1. **Your Lifetime Objectives**–Imagine a man-on-the-street interviewer for a television show shoving a microphone in front of you. "You will win one million dollars," he says, "if you have written down your lifetime objectives. Ah-ah-ah! No fair writing them on the spot!" How much will you win? Rate yourself on a scale of 1 to 10.

   1—+—+—+—+—+—+—+—+—10

   Not one cent — A $1 million jackpot

2. **Your Organizational Mission and Vision**–The same man-on-the-street interviewer offers you another million if you can accurately explain your organization's mission and objectives. Saying, "But nobody ever told me!" does not count. Can you explain it or not? That is all the interviewer wants to know. How much will you win?

   1—+—+—+—+—+—+—+—+—10

   Zilch — The full $1 million

3. **Your Three-Year Objectives**–How clear and specific are the goals and mental word pictures for what you want to accomplish during the next three years?

   1—+—+—+—+—+—+—+—+—10

   I've been meaning to get around to that. — They are clear and specific.

4. **Your One-Year Targets for Each Priority Area**–Do you have clear, written goals for where you want to be one year from now in each important area of your life?

   1—+—+—+—+—+—+—+—+—10

   Could we change the subject? — I have them all written out.

CONTINUED

CONTINUED

5. **Your Dream**–Do you have a dream that is so important to you that whenever you have a spare moment, your thoughts automatically turn to ways to accomplish that dream? (Your dream may already be in your lifetime objectives or your organizational mission.)

1——+——+——+——+——+——+——+——+——10

I'm just trying to survive the day. | My dream pulls me through life.

6. **Your Passion**–Do you support a cause that is bigger than yourself, your family, or your friends? Is it a cause to which you devote time and energy each week?

1——+——+——+——+——+——+——+——+——10

I wish I did. | Oh, yes! The most wonderful cause in the world!

Answer Key: The Power of Purpose

Reflect on your answers. Were your winnings and your ratings as high as you want them? If your answer is:

Yes.

Congratulate yourself. You are among a select group of achievers. You have a head start on getting everything you want in life. Plus, you have a head start on being a valued person in the lives of your family, friends, employers, employees, and customers.

No.

Are you embarrassed by some of your answers to these questions? Worry not. You don't have to reveal them to anyone else. This exercise is for your benefit. It helps you get a better picture of your life–your stress level and your motivation level. You are now among those select few who have a better understanding of their own motivation level. That understanding is a big doorway to taking purposeful action for improvement.

Now go back through the questions. Imagine yourself scoring at the high end of each scale. Picture how good it feels to have a clear direction and purpose in life. Then commit yourself to taking whatever action is needed to build your passionate sense of direction and motivation.

For Extra Credit

The lights over a stadium at night are no brighter than the lights you have in your life with up-to-date answers to the questions. Most people need time to think through the answers to the man-on-the-street interview.

When is a likely day and time for you to carve out some good thinking time?

____

____

What is a timetable for completion that will motivate you?

____

____

It is never too late to do this thinking, as you will see in the next case study.

Stress and the Motivational Power of a Dream

"A *dream did it."* Carol smiled musingly at the group around the table as she shared a story from her family experience. "A dream helped my 79-year-old father-in-law survive tremendous stress," she said. "I believe it was his dream that pulled him through to his 80th birthday.

"The doctors told us Pops was living on oxygen and borrowed time and that he had only a few more weeks to live. I remembered how he always enjoyed having a dream or big goal to work toward. So that evening I sat down beside his bed in our upstairs bedroom, and I threw him a challenge: 'Pops, how about hosting a birthday party for yourself a year from now? Invite the five kids and their families. You know, Pops, you can't take it with you. Why don't you pay for the party and the travel for everyone too?'

"Even though he was weak and on oxygen most of the time, Pops spent the entire year planning the food, checking which grandchild wanted to share a room with whom, fine-tuning the schedule, organizing awards for the basketball contest, and tracking down the best air fares. I saw him literally pulled through that last year by his dream.

"To the doctors' amazement, Pops made it to his 80th birthday party. That dream gave us all the pleasure of an extra year of his life."

A strong motivational draw helps us punch through times of stress. Whether we are in our 20s, 40s, 60s, or 80s, a powerful sense of direction and purpose can add to our enjoyment, our productivity, and our lifespan.

Wrap-Up for Part 2

As you read the stress and motivation insights in this part, you probably discovered some that were especially meaningful and relevant to you. To fortify your recall, check (✔) those points below:

- ❑ I can prevent stress by being alert to the early warning signals.
- ❑ Language can multiply or subtract feelings of stress.
- ❑ I can bring stress factors into balance by giving myself a clear sense of purpose, direction, and passion in life.

In the next part you will discover a shortcut for getting a new and powerful perspective on stress factors.

PART 3

Purposeful Self-Talk: A Great Place to Start

"*Sow a thought, and you reap an act;*
Sow an act, and you reap a habit;
Sow a habit, and you reap a character;
Sow a character, and you reap a destiny."

–Samuel Smiles

SUCCESS SECRET

When you want a change, there is an easy and effective way to start. Change what you say to yourself.

The Power of Purposeful Self-Talk

In the next few pages, you will discover new dimensions in the power of what you say to yourself. You will explore:

- What happens when you instill purpose in what you say to yourself
- Ways to use purposeful self-talk to save time, feel better, and get the right things done
- How repetition wins
- The relationship between self-talk and feelings

Firestorm or Fireplace

By now it is very clear: What we say to ourselves about our situation will either stress or motivate us. How tragic that so few people really understand this fundamental dynamic.

Left unattended, self-talk can turn into a raging firestorm of negativity. When a wildfire races out of control, flames leap from tree to tree, housetop to housetop. Houses explode in flames and are destroyed in seconds.

Negative, unattended self-talk can be just as devastating in a person's life as that firestorm. It destroys creativity. It damages confidence. It degrades productivity. It becomes a self-fulfilling prophecy of doom and gloom, an ever-worsening feedback loop of discouragement.

But when self-talk is directed, contained, and purposeful, it provides light and warmth–just like the cozy, soothing blaze in a fireplace. Hold that picture in your mind for a moment. Think of yourself sitting in front of a fireplace on a rainy evening. Breathe in the redolence of the burning logs. Feel the warmth of the glowing coals. Consider how protected and safe you feel next to that dancing fire while the cold wind rattles the tree branches outside.

Fireplace or firestorm–it is the same power. But what a difference. In the fireplace, that power is contained. It has a place. It has purpose. It is controlled.

Self-talk is a power like fire. Left uncontrolled, it can destroy. But take charge of it, direct it, give it purpose, and it can profoundly change your life for the better.

Stress from Downers and Drainers

The following experiment shows how words shape your feelings and influence your behavior. The statements below take just minutes to read, but you may be surprised at the impact they make on your thinking and feeling.

As you read these stressful and unproductive self-talk statements, be aware of your feelings. You will get the most from this experiment if you read the sentences aloud.

I can't stand it.

I just can't deal with it anymore.

I feel terrible.

I just don't know what to do.

I'm always so far behind.

That is so stupid.

I shouldn't have to do this.

I'm just waiting for someone to notice.

There is too much to do.

Nobody appreciates me.

Everyone is so uncooperative.

There's nothing I can do.

Practice

On a scale of 1 to 10, rate yourself on the following questions.

1. How do you feel?

1—+—+—+—+—+—+—+—+—10

Drained. Discouraged. Great! Top of the world.

2. How energized are you to take constructive action?

1—+—+—+—+—+—+—+—+—10

Tired. Blah. I need a nap. I'm going to move mountains.

3. After reading the downers and drainers list, how likely are you to make continuous improvements in your life?

1—+—+—+—+—+—+—+—+—10

I pass. You can count on me.

Adding Motivation with Lifters and Leaders

Now read this second list–aloud, if possible–and be aware of your thinking and feeling responses as you read.

I always have choices.

There is always something I can do.

I turn problems into opportunities.

I keep myself in a good mood.

I picture what I want in wonderful detail.

I "grab 15." It is incredible how much I can accomplish in 15 minutes.

I finish fully and I feel good.

I forgive and I feel free.

This is a good day.

I help people get what they want.

I ask for what I want.

I take good care of myself.

I prevent problems.

I solve problems without blaming others or myself.

I do it now.

I give myself a great start because I wrap up the tough top priority first.

Practice

Now take your *mental pulse.* Tune in to your feelings and your thoughts. On a scale of 1 to 10, rate yourself on the following questions:

1. How do you feel?

1———+———+———+———+———+———+———+———+———10

Drained. Discouraged. Great! Top of the world.

2. How energized are you to take constructive action?

1———+———+———+———+———+———+———+———+———10

Tired. Blah. I need a nap. I'm going to move mountains.

3. How likely are you to make continuous improvements in your life?

1———+———+———+———+———+———+———+———+———10

I pass. You can count on me.

There is no question which list leaves you feeling the best, feeling productive, feeling energized to take on the world.

Three Important Questions About Self-Talk

Perhaps you are thinking there must be more to this self-talk concept than just talking to yourself. Indeed, there is. The answers to the three questions that follow will help you understand this powerful technique for motivating yourself to take productive action.

Question 1: What Makes Self-Talk Work?

The key is purposeful action. Rather than letting random ideas float around in every direction, shape your self-talk around the purposes you select. That is what makes them motivational. Make sure everything you say to yourself contributes to where you want to go. And make sure your self-talk encourages you to take action.

You can employ two kinds of purposeful self-talk to reinforce the goals you have chosen:

- Word pictures that describe the objectives and destinations you want to reach

- Processes, or repetitive steps, that help you reach your desired destinations

Here's an example of how these two forms of purposeful self-talk work. Barbara used a word picture to imagine herself at her goal weight, wearing a size-6 red dress. She also used the process of telling herself, "When I feel tempted to graze, I reach for some carrot sticks." The combination of these two enabled her to reach her objective. You will tap into the power of word pictures more fully in Part 7.

Question 2: Don't You Have to Do More Than Just Say Things to Yourself?

The answer is a loud and clear yes. Self-talk is merely the beginning. Improving what you say to yourself is not the end–more productive action is.

Think of it this way: Self-talk that does not produce productive action is like buying a boat and leaving it tied up at the dock. Productive behavior is the ultimate goal of purposeful self-talk, just as an enjoyable sail on the lake is the ultimate goal of buying a boat.

Purposeful thinking prompts purposeful behavior.

Purposeful self-talk is a way to train yourself to do the right thing at the right time. Plant constructive ideas in your mind over and over. Nurture them and they will grow. The ideas become habits. Then when the opportunity comes, you automatically say the right thing to yourself. This in turn encourages you to do the right thing.

The case study on the next page shows how one person changed her behavior by first changing her thinking.

The Scavenger Hunt

R*achael described herself as a street-savvy woman* who had worked her way up through the ranks to a responsible job. But she confessed she struggled with clutter every day. "I waste so much time looking for things," she said self-reproachfully. "You wouldn't believe the stacks of paper on my desk. And the stacks on the table. And my file drawers are a disaster."

Every day, big chunks of Rachael's time were chewed up by "scavenger hunts." She might have misplaced a letter, a file folder, some receipts, her keys, her earrings–it was always something. She fumed about the wasted time, but until now, did not know how to solve the problem.

"Two months ago, I misplaced some travel receipts. After almost two hours of fruitless searching, I threw up my hands and said, 'Enough is enough!' I suddenly realized that I actually knew the answer. I was just not doing the things that I knew would help me. When I was a kid, my mother always told me, 'A place for everything and everything in its place.' Every time she told me that, I would grind my teeth!

"I started repeating to myself an idea I had heard in a seminar: 'No temporary parking places–in place or in use.' I wrote that idea on a three-by-five card and kept it by my computer. I repeated the idea to myself morning, noon, and night. I even pictured myself with a fistful of $20 bills from turning in my receipts and expenses.

"It's funny. After picturing the cash in hand and reading that sign to myself for only a month, I started to change what I did. I would almost be ready to toss a folder on a pile on my desk or stuff a receipt in my coat pocket–and then I would smile and encourage myself 'No temporary parking places. In place or in use!' Then I would walk to the filing cabinet and slip that folder into its regular parking place. Or I would put that receipt in the right pocket in my wallet.

"Clutter has always been such a hassle for me. Now it's almost fun finding ways to keep myself organized. And I am spending less and less time on 'scavenger hunts'!"

The key: Purposeful thinking really does prompt purposeful behavior.

Question 3: But Aren't You Telling Yourself Something That Isn't True?

You are saying it on faith. The book of Hebrews defines it this way: "Faith is being sure of what we hope for and certain of what we do not see." When you plant your hope of future results in the present, you exercise your faith. It is like picturing a full-grown oak tree when you plant an acorn in the ground.

You add the energizing element of faith when you actively state and affirm a hope as if it has already happened. And repetition compels faith.

Repetition Wins

Advertising companies have understood the power of repetition for decades. Winning the race for top position in people's minds depends on repetition. No one deliberately decides to learn the messages that advertisers broadcast our way, yet chances are each of us knows how to finish a popular slogan or jingle.

Brian's Story

Repetition invariably makes a profound impact–whether for good or bad. Brian was a seven-year-old boy, exuberant and lovable. One evening, as his mother was helping him with his addition, Brian shoved his books across the kitchen table and grumped, "Just forget it, Mom! I'm stupid. I can't do math."

Even though the standardized tests at school show a strong aptitude for math, Brian scores Ds in his arithmetic class. Even though he is a bright child, his self-talk is tearing him down. He repeats to himself, "I'm stupid. I can't do math." Worst of all, he is putting his belief into action.

Repetition does win–and tragically so, in Brian's case.

We Become What We Think About

We do become what we think about. This is hardly a new idea–although it is a much-neglected one. Purposeful self-talk reinforces the best in us so that we can *do* our best and be our best.

Wrap-Up for Part 3

Let's bring home the key realities of this part. Check (✔) the ideas that are the most important and helpful to you:

- ❑ What I say to myself is either a fireplace or a firestorm. I am talking to myself all the time, so it makes sense to say things that are helpful.
- ❑ Some statements drain energy and trigger stress.
- ❑ Other statements lift, direct, and motivate.
- ❑ When I put purpose into my self-talk, I triple the benefits.
- ❑ Self-talk is not the goal. Its value lies in the purposeful action it prompts.
- ❑ Repetition is not a luxury. It is a necessity for winning. I can train myself for success by repeating positive, purposeful reinforcements.
- ❑ Starting an improvement with self-talk makes sense because it is effective and totally within my control, and it takes only minutes a day.

In the next part, you will see how to become your own best coach through purposeful self-talk.

PART 4

Stress Reduction: The Self-Coaching Process

> *"Winning isn't everything—but wanting to win is."*
>
> –Coach Vince Lombardi

SUCCESS SECRET

Be your own coach. Whether you are ahead or behind, keep on coaching yourself.

What If Others Are Causing Your Stress?

This question pops up first in seminars on stress. And it is easy to see why this is such a common concern. In a stressful situation, it is natural to respond, "Someone else needs to change, or this situation needs to change. If only the circumstances were different, I wouldn't have this stress." In times of stress it is much harder to say, "I need to change."

It is a paradox. If we follow our instincts and try to change other people, our stress will actually increase. But when we make a decision to change ourselves and take action toward a solution, we become stronger and the stress loses its power over us. And then there is often a fringe benefit. Once people stop pressuring others and start solving their part of the problem, the other people often change.

To change ourselves in times of stress, we need to become our own coaches. We need to learn to talk to ourselves so we can turn our external stress factors into internal motivation for change and improvement.

In this part, you will be hearing about self-coaching. Most of the principles you will gain in this part come from the example of Doug. Through his story, you will polish your skills in these areas:

- What to do when confronted by difficult people
- How to fix your part of the problem without owning the other person's part
- How to use self-coaching techniques to tackle stress

As you read and do the exercises, remember: Good coaches do not give up just because the team is down a few points. Good coaches are there for the wins *and* the losses. Never give up on yourself! Keep on coaching yourself whether you are winning or losing. Use the powerful techniques of self-coaching and enjoy the benefits of reduced stress, increased power, stronger relationships, and more effective motivation.

Warm-Up Exercise

To get the most from the case study in this part, first spend a few moments concentrating on your story.

1. Describe a particularly stressful time in your life.

2. What did you do in that situation to turn it around? In reflecting on that turnaround, what did you do to help yourself recover from that stressful experience?

3. What lessons did you learn from that situation?

Now read Doug's story on the following pages as he shares his time of stress, his turnaround experience, and his personal paradigm shift–the enhancement in his thinking that enabled him to pull out of his stressful nosedive.

Doug's Story: Stress and All Those Turkeys

"I *never said I had a stress problem. I said I had a turkey problem,"* Doug announced. "Turkeys in traffic," he grumbled. "Turkeys in management. Too many turkeys. Everyone taking a piece out of me. I just want the people around me to stop acting like a big bunch of inconsiderate turkeys."

In bits and pieces Doug revealed his story. A sales representative for an electronics company, he was struggling with professional burnout, complicated by a 20-year marriage gone stale and the pressures of raising two teenage boys. Anger and futility had trapped him in a vise grip of stressful resentment day after day.

"People at work are so out to lunch. Getting ahead around here–it's all politics. They made me a sales manager two years ago. After a month, I told them to keep it. Transfer me back to being a sales rep."

More Motivated

Doug clenched and unclenched his teeth as he continued. "Last week my boss sat down with me and gave me another talk about how I need to be more motivated. I thought to myself, 'Yeah, I sure do need more motivation and just exactly when was he going to motivate me? What a jerk!' Turkeys all day long, and then I get it from my boss and then from my wife when I get home. It isn't fair.

"Sometimes I think the only appreciation I get is from my golden retriever, Goldie. As soon as I walk in the door, I head for that dog and we have us a good wrestling match. My wife, Brenda, has a fit. Says our rough play sends a cloud of dog hair floating over the couches and chairs. She says I should take the dog outside. I can hear her now. Nag, nag, nag. She complains to our sons, 'I don't know how long your dad expects me to put up with his antics. Here he is–rushes into the house, makes a mess, wolfs down his food and takes off. Dirty dishes and dog hair. That's how you know he's been here!'"

Doug chuckled mirthlessly. "Funny, huh? All I get from my wife is static. Nothing is good enough for her. She's always trying to change me. What does she want–perfection? No wonder I'm outta there every chance I get to coach my son's basketball team. We're in last place, but we are going to turn things around. I keep on telling those kids, 'You can do it.' Then I see something sink in and they get out there and do it. When a kid calls, 'Heeeey Coach,' that's the best! Brenda nags me about the time I spend on basketball, but coaching the kids is *the only place I'm a hero.*"

Pressures Plus

"Between my boss and my wife, I've had it.

"I know my job's on the line. Sales are down. But everyone is having quota problems. What do you expect with all these rumors about consolidations and cutbacks? Sure, I'm getting a few complaint calls. I don't have time to follow up on every little detail. With all the meetings and paperwork, how does the company expect me to sell anything? Sure, I tell myself to stop procrastinating on the paperwork, but I feel buried sometimes. I have to put up with piles of garbage.

"Day after day I'm out there by myself dealing with inconsiderate turkeys. I don't dare talk back to customers. And I can't say anything to my boss. I just have to keep on eating it. Yesterday I got so ticked off, I felt like my head was going to explode."

Doug slumped down in his chair. "But it's not just my head I'm afraid of losing. If things don't change, I may lose my job, and my wife. Everything."

The Turning Point

"Remember the other day when I said things had to change? Well, it's beginning to sink in that maybe I'm the one who needs to change." Doug sat down, this time looking more relaxed. The stress lines in his forehead were less furrowed.

"I had a doctor appointment, and he told me I had to work on getting over feeling down. He said I was already doing the most important thing–exercising. He got out his little white notepad and prescribed three things:

- ➤ Be more forgiving and less irritated.
- ➤ Ask for what you want rather than not saying anything and resenting everything.
- ➤ Talk about your feelings rather than slamming doors.

"You can imagine how I hate that 'get in the hot tub and talk about your feelings' stuff. The doc did say that I will be able to control my feelings better when I put them into words. I don't know about that. But I know I have to do something. Maybe I should try that seminar on stress and self-talk that my boss has been trying to shove down my throat. I know I need something."

Coaching Yourself

"Soon after that, I sat cooling my heels in a customer's reception area. I picked up a golf magazine. As I was thumbing through it, an article about my favorite pro caught my eye. He described how he said things to himself to keep his concentration each game. The idea looked different. More sports related. Well, I ripped out the article and stuck it in my coat pocket.

"A week later I stopped at a coffee shop about eleven o'clock in the morning to get organized. I was fishing through my briefcase and came across that article. I ended up sitting there and reading for 45 minutes. Then it struck me.

"What that article was talking about is coaching yourself.

"I finally said, 'I have nothing to lose. I'm in trouble, and this might work. I'll give it a try.' I copied a dozen of the ideas into the time organizer the company gave me."

"Well, I never looked in that section of my organizer again. So the next time, I put the reinforcements on cards. Then somehow I couldn't find the cards. So I went out for another cup of coffee, put the ideas together again–this time on Post-it® notes that I stuck on a file folder. Then that night, I unfolded it and read the ideas onto a tape that I use in my car. I figure I can listen to it while I buzz along the freeway heading for my appointments. Who knows? Maybe they'll help somehow."

Noticing a Difference

"Hey, it sounds weak, but I am noticing a difference." His voice was buoyant and without its usual edge of sarcasm. "Like, when people start acting like turkeys, I think about some of those ideas on my tape. I've stopped saying so many negative things to myself. That makes it easier to deal with the negative things others say to me. I don't use all the ideas yet, but I know my life will be a lot smoother when I do. Listening to those ideas does calm me down and keep me on course. Here are *some* of my winners:

- When things get tough, I keep coaching myself.
- I can lose the game and still win the championship.
- The playing field doesn't always have to be level.
- It's all right when life isn't fair.
- Doug, you can do it, too.

"I still haven't quite gotten to the place where I can accept 'I talk about feelings,' but I think I'm getting there. I'm doing other hard things. When I'm driving, I picture myself blocking in my weekly sales plan before four on Friday. I see myself asking for the order and closing. Frankly, this whole idea blows my mind. I didn't think what I said to myself made any difference. I used to think other people were the problem. But I guess I was wrong.

"I've discovered that using a self-talk system has helped me. I have a better attitude at work and better communications with my wife. Now I don't expect my manager to motivate me. That never worked anyway. I know that my motivation is my responsibility. And these days, when I get home, I hug my wife first, not Goldie. I know that used to bug Brenda. Now I hug her and tell her about my day.

"The other evening she asked, 'Doug, what happened? You're not down like you used to be. And you are not talking about turkeys all the time. When you smile now, your eyes smile too.' I could tell by her expression that she really likes what I'm doing. You know, I've been thinking that maybe someday I'll let her listen to my tape."

Coach Talk

Doug started out a doubter and ended up a fan of purposeful self-talk and self-coaching. The principles he learned can be used by all of us to increase our effectiveness and satisfaction in life.

The key principle he discovered was to coach yourself. Find the repetition method that works for you and use it. For some people, the best method may be three-by-five-inch cards, Post-it notes, or a computer file. For Doug, it was a cassette tape and his car's tape player.

On his tapes, Doug recorded such coach talk as, "You can lose the game and still win the championship" and "The playing field does not always have to be level."

Here are other suggestions for coaching yourself:

- Most people are fair.
- Life has given me a lot.
- People have given me a lot.
- I keep score on the good things I have.
- When I have a problem with someone, I fix my part of the problem.
- I forgive and I move ahead.
- I ask for what I want.
- I assist people in getting what they want.
- I am a most valuable player.
- You are a most valuable player.
- I find ways to help everyone win.
- I ask for the order and I close.
- I put papers away right away.
- I do it anyway.
- I do it now.

For more ideas, read Be Your Own Coach *by Barbara Braham and Christine Wahl, Crisp Publications.*

Cool-Down Exercise

Now it is time to make the transition from Doug's story to your story. As you reflect on Doug's experience, consider these questions:

1. With which parts of Doug's story did you identify?

 ____

2. What did you learn or reinforce?

 ____

3. After reading Doug's story, what would you be encouraged to do more frequently? (For example, take action rather than waiting for someone to motivate you.)

 ____

Now consider these questions about your own story:

4. Assume you are coaching yourself. You are standing alongside the playing field of your daily challenges. As an objective but caring coach, you watch yourself handle the stresses and challenges of life and your career. How would you describe yourself as a player?

 ____

5. As your coach, what words of encouragement would you call out?

 ____

6. Now rewrite those words of encouragement into clear, positive statements you can repeat to yourself as reinforcements–that is, as purposeful self-talk you can listen to every day:

 ____

One of the primary functions of a coach is to motivate players to persevere and give maximum effort in preparation for the game getting tough. It is an important job. So accept the job. Be your own best coach every day. Don't wait for others to change. Make changes where they really count–within yourself.

Every time you do this, you will be moving toward where you want to be and doing what you want to do.

Wrap-Up for Part 4

To assist you in getting the most value from this part, check (✔) the ideas that have the most meaning and relevance to you:

- ❑ I reduce stress most effectively when I stop blaming others for my problems.
- ❑ My best strategy for stress reduction and increased motivation is to objectively and positively coach myself with purposeful self-talk.
- ❑ If I get into trouble, I do what any good coach does; I stick with it. I keep on coaching myself, even in stressful times.
- ❑ If I have a problem with someone, I fix my part of the problem.
- ❑ When a system or process does not work for me, I put together a process that does.
- ❑ I take successes in one area of my life and apply them to other areas.

In the next part, you will discover powerful techniques for an issue practically everyone wants to get in shape–procrastination.

PART 5

Procrastination and Motivation: Four Great Techniques

> "*Do what you can, with what you have, where you are.*"
>
> –Theodore Roosevelt

SUCCESS SECRET

Do it now!

Talking Yourself Out of Procrastination

The conference room was filled with 500 of the most successful executives and managers in American business. The question raised was, How many of you are procrastinating in some area of your life? Hands shot up all over the room. At least 400 of the 500 participants answered with a raised hand, "Yes, I have a problem with procrastination."

People who procrastinate are not alone. Practically everyone procrastinates at some time–even on projects they know will benefit them.

Procrastination-Proofing Techniques

There is good news in this part for times of procrastination. In the coming pages we will explore practical strategies and shortcuts that have been proven to work by hundreds of people. We will discover how the guilt and discouragement of procrastination can be transformed into the satisfaction of getting the right things done.

Take a closer look at these powerful techniques for procrastination-proofing yourself.

Technique 1: Grab 15

This classic technique for overcoming procrastination heads the popularity list every time. You will be amazed at what you can accomplish by working on a job at least 15 minutes a day.

For most people the hardest part of conquering procrastination is getting started. When you promise yourself that your commitment is for only 15 minutes, it's much easier to get started. One man even made one of his reinforcements "I can do anything for 15 minutes!"

Consider what you can accomplish by consistently investing 15 minutes a day:

- Write a manual
- Learn a new language in three years
- Remodel a room
- Read the entire Bible in a year
- Catch up on paperwork
- Learn a new computer application
- Grow a small garden
- Learn to read financial reports
- Flatten your stomach

Charlotte Hale saw tangible proof of this powerful technique when she and her husband visited a friend in a small southern town. Their friend was the town's only doctor and the new owner of a rambling house that had been vacant for years. When they arrived, their friend was standing in the middle of a room with paint cans and tools scattered across the floor. He looked at the ceiling and declared, "That has got to come down." They thought he was merely dreaming until he took them into his new bathroom. The ceiling was lowered. New cabinets were installed. New plumbing was in place. He smiled as he pointed with pride to the heated towel bar he had installed.

When they asked how he did it, he smiled again and said, "It's simple. I work at least 15 minutes a day, every day, without fail."

Grab 15 can help you tackle those projects at work that have been falling behind.

15 Minutes a Day Equals 78 Hours a Year

The magic of the Grab 15 technique is that 15 minutes a day, day after day, quickly adds up. Even if you take Sunday off, you can chalk up 90 productive minutes a week. Just look:

15 minutes x 6 days = 90 minutes a week

90 minutes a week x 52 weeks = 4,680 minutes or 78 hours

Imagine what you could accomplish if someone waved a wand and magically gave you 78 extra hours! The Grab 15 technique puts that magic wand in your own hands. Here are additional benefits of the Grab 15 technique:

The Creativity Benefit

When you work on a task for 15 minutes a day, that task is always simmering on the back burner of your mind. Imagine walking into a kitchen where there is a pan of spiced apple cider on the stove gently heating on the back burner. The aroma is everywhere. So is your creativity when you commit to Grab 15. Even when you are not consciously thinking about the job, your subconscious is working for you. You discover unexpected resources and new ways to streamline your tasks. You think and work more creatively.

The Bonus Benefit

Some days, after you finish your 15-minute commitment, you will be on a roll. You will feel like continuing. And you will. That bonus effort will bring you that much closer to your goal.

Add to your motivation by telling yourself, "I Grab 15."

Practice

Test it yourself:

1. Pick a big job that is sliding behind schedule or any task of any size for which you have not been able to find time.
2. Commit yourself to working on that task at least 15 minutes a day. Decide, when is the best time of day to carve out that 15 minutes?
3. Consider how you can reward yourself for your consistency. It could be anything from a star on your calendar to a gift for yourself, perhaps a book you've been wanting to read or a CD you have been wanting to enjoy.

Technique 2: Do the Toughest Top Priority First

Tackle that important but unpleasant task first and get it out of the way. Have you ever had a day when, as you drive to work, you are thinking about the job that has to be done, but that job is the last thing you want to do? Have you noticed that the longer you put it off, the more it haunts you and will not let you forget it? It hovers over you like a gray cloud. If you move away from your desk, it follows you. When the phone rings, you hope it is not someone wondering if that tough top-priority job is done.

Now picture this: As you drive to work, you think about that tough top-priority task and you flex your mental muscles. Arriving at your desk, you meet that task head-on. It may be a report you have been putting off, a bad-news phone call you need to make, that correspondence you need to answer. Whatever it is, as soon as you get it done, the whole world lights up. That gray cloud floats away. You feel your life is under control. You feel energized.

Is there something on your mind that needs to be done, but that you don't feel like doing? If so, give it a name:______________________________

Next, give yourself a lift. Picture yourself getting that job done and out of your life.

Now make that picture a reality. Tackle that job now.

Technique 3: Keep Your Stimulation and Excitement Quota Full

Many people procrastinate because they thrive on the challenge of getting things done under last-minute pressure. Such individuals have a high *stimulation and excitement quota.* They regularly end up getting things done at the last minute. If it is 8 A.M. and they have a report due at 4 P.M. and the report preparation takes an hour, you can predict that these people will start on the report at 3 P.M.–or maybe 3:15. It is more exciting that way. If such individuals inadvertently get caught up on their work before a trip or an event, they will feel compelled to add a new project.

The solution is to keep your stimulation and excitement quota filled productively. This reduces the need to fill your quota by procrastination. If you know you like a lot of excitement, plan for it. Have lunch with a new person, take on a new assignment, join an extra professional association, learn a new software application. You know what appeals to your personality. Keep your S&EQ at the level you want. Reinforce yourself with these self-talk statements:

- I plan for a good amount of excitement in my life.
- I keep my stimulation and excitement quota filled in positive ways.

If you identify with the high stimulation and excitement quota, you can read an entire chapter on this dynamic in How to Put More Time in Your Life, *by Dru Scott.*

Technique 4: Face Up to the Feeling

Procrastination can be a way of avoiding feelings–most often feelings of success, enjoyment, or closeness. Many people procrastinate to avoid the feeling they would have if they finished the task–not just to avoid the task itself. Consider how these statements could show up in procrastination:

"I wouldn't know what to do if I got caught up."

"If I got caught up on my work, it would scare me to death."

"I feel needed when I have a lot of work to do."

If you see some connections, consider using these self-talk reinforcements:

"I accept what I am feeling without trying to cover it with work."

"My feelings are okay."

"I talk about my feelings because that helps me control them."

"It is okay for me to feel ..." [the feeling you may be avoiding]

Pick the procrastination techniques that reduce stress and build your motivation.

Wrap-Up for Part 5

Check (✔) the techniques that are most important to you:

- ❑ I keep procrastination in its place with the four proven techniques.
- ❑ I "Grab 15." It is incredible how much I can accomplish in 15 minutes.
- ❑ I energize myself because I tackle the toughest top priority first.
- ❑ I keep my stimulation and excitement quota filled positively.
- ❑ I face up to my feelings. My feelings are okay.

In the next part you will explore a powerful system to motivate yourself. The system will help you generate motivation beyond your wildest dreams.

P A R T 6

Mega Motivation with Pictures of Excellence

"*Where there is no vision, the people perish.*"

–Proverbs 29:18

SUCCESS SECRET

Because we are motivated by what we are missing, why not put this reality to work? Picture what you want in photographic detail.

We Are Motivated by What We Are Missing

"I have the best nose money can buy," Teri explained as she chuckled and slipped off her glasses so everyone in the seminar could get a good look at her nose. "You talk about being motivated by what you are missing. I am an example. I have a beautiful nose now, but this is not my original nose."

Teri by a Nose

"You should have seen me when I was in school," she explained. "As soon as I started first grade, I became self-conscious about my nose. It was big with a definite hook. Kids in my class called me 'The Beak' and 'Honker.' If I were to show you my school pictures, you'd see why the kids teased me. It was a major nose!

"Throughout my school years, it was all I thought about. I wore long bangs in a futile attempt to detract from it. I begged to wear glasses. I did everything I could to make my nose less noticeable. I used to dream what it would be like to have a small nose. I imagined striding into a room, shoulders back, chin up, flashing my new nose.

"Finally, when I was 25, my husband and I agreed I was going to have cosmetic surgery. At last, I was going to have the nose I had imagined for so many years. After the surgery, the doctor removed the bandages from my nose. I looked in the mirror. The skin was still tender and red, but I knew my nose was going to be beautiful! It was exactly the size and shape I had dreamed about since I was a kid!

"Only moments later as I held the mirror and admired my nose, I saw something that I had never, ever noticed before. Not my nose–my *teeth.* For the first time, I noticed the gap between my two front teeth. My dream of a beautiful nose had come true–yet within seconds, I forgot the nose I had been obsessed with for almost 20 years! Now, I was motivated by that gap between my two front teeth!"

Teri's story is a memorable example of this reality: We are motivated by what we are missing.

Motivational Power with Pictures

How can you put this reality to work? Develop a picture in your mind. You will start missing that picture. For example, if you picture yourself at your new desk, dealing with your new responsibilities and collecting that new, bigger paycheck, then you will "miss" that new job and be motivated by it.

We can harness the pulling power of mental pictures to motivate us toward our achievable goals. The way to harness the power of these pictures is by learning to picture what you want in vivid detail. Unbelievable motivating power exists in imagining *pictures of excellence.*

Turning your targets, objectives, and dreams into pictures of excellence helps you miss them. Picturing the finished result you want triggers the missing effect and adds to your motivation. Expressing the results you desire in pictures gives you an extra supply of drive and discipline. Here are some examples:

Picture of Excellence 1: Jerry, a do-it-yourself carpenter in his spare time, pictures the family room addition he wants to build on his house. He imagines it in great detail–comfortable couch in front of a stone fireplace, a big-screen TV in the corner, his three children laughing and munching popcorn as they enjoy the spacious new addition.

Picture of Excellence 2: Devona keeps herself motivated in her sales engineering job by picturing that high-end, high-tech packaging system already installed and running in her customer's plant. She sees her customer's employees standing beside the system, measuring how rapidly it runs and how much time and money it is saving.

Picture of Excellence 3: Barbara pictures herself at her goal weight. She is standing in front of a mirror wearing a red dress in size 6.

These different people in different situations make their lives more satisfying and their organizations more effective by picturing what they want. Detailed pictures of excellence put enormous motivational power in our heads and in our hands. They encourage us to take action.

Why Do Pictures of Excellence Work So Powerfully?

You read in the examples on the previous page how different people pictured what they wanted to achieve, which then added to their motivation in making that picture come true. But you may be wondering about the power behind these pictures of excellence. They work by:

- **Providing right-brain involvement.**
  Pictures involve the visual, spatial, creative properties of the right brain, not just the cognitive properties of the left brain. So often statements of purpose and direction appeal only to the left brain. Pictures of excellence add the power appeal of the right-brain hemisphere.

- **Giving your objectives the appeal of the emotional first brain.**
  Exciting new information shows that pictures directly affect our more primitive brain first, even before they reach the left and right hemispheres. In his book, *You've Got To Be Believed To Be Heard,* author Bert Decker writes about the *First Brain,* which is our emotional brain (the limbic system). It is that primitive and unconscious part of the brain that is a powerful driving force in our lives. The First Brain is directly affected by all of our sensory input. What you see and hear is literally transmitted through the First Brain even before it reaches the left and right hemispheres of the *New Brain,* the cerebral cortex. Although the First Brain is affected by all senses, it is very much dominated by the visual input. Which is why visualizing pictures can have an even more powerful impact than ever thought possible.

Traditionally, when leaders wanted to communicate the organization's goals to the troops, they used words, logic, rationales, facts, and analyses designed to appeal to the thinking brain (cerebral cortex). But facts and figures reach only the conscious and only the left side of the conscious brain at that. It is easy to see why so many people lose interest and nod off during traditional meetings.

Facts and logic inform; they do not inspire. They do not excite. They do not activate our emotional brain. Paint a picture, however, and you add the pulling power of the emotional First Brain.

Using Word Pictures as Reinforcements

Actual pictures work the best, but not everyone can draw or has an actual picture. You may need to "draw" the picture with words before you can see it in your mind. Then when you say the words, the picture flashes onto the screen of your mind.

A Great Place to Work

You can use word pictures to focus your team or organization on achieving a common goal. Here are two ways pictures can motivate and make your organization a great place to work.

Teamwork with Shared Pictures of Excellence

When you help your group visualize a picture that represents group success, you give people a priceless gift–direction and motivation. Often goals and objectives come across to employees as a collection of cold words and numbing figures. A vivid, detailed picture of excellence plants a common vision of success in the minds of everyone. It unifies them and pulls them in the same direction. Groups move forward more rapidly when their leaders unite them around a shared picture of where the group is going. Leadership means communicating a shared picture of excellence.

- ➤ Bill, the head of an information systems department, inspires his staff with this word picture: "Imagine a group of company people around a table discussing a decision. Thanks to us, that group has the right information at the right time in the right form at the right place."

- ➤ Mary, the vice president of a 600-bed medical center, shares this word picture with her nursing staff: "A man is leaving our outpatient treatment facility, and he is saying to the person picking him up, 'The people at the medical center are wonderful. They gave me great care and there were no surprises.'"

Self-Management with Shared Pictures of Excellence

When each person in a group can picture and describe where the group wants to go, you encourage self-management. People make better decisions when they know why and where they are going. A big reason for poor decisions, lack of motivation, and lack of initiative is that people do not clearly understand where the group is going and why.

Three Success Secrets

As you have read in examples and explanations, pictures of excellence can work powerfully to motivate us toward our achievable goals. You will gain the most motivational value by applying the following three recommendations:

1. Make your word pictures snapshot-specific.

Fill your word pictures with vivid detail. Make them as specific as an actual photograph.

2. Find a word picture for each priority area.

If an area of your life is important to you, find a picture to represent where you want to go with it.

- If you're working on a cost-reduction program, picture the pizza party to celebrate reaching your cost-reduction goals.

- If you want a strong marriage, find a picture that represents what you will be doing and enjoying in your strong marriage, perhaps sitting at a table discussing problems peacefully and working out solutions. Or picture going out to a candlelight dinner for a special date with your spouse.

Practice

Write a word picture for each of your five or six priority areas on the job and at home. Use your word pictures as the basis for your gallery of mental pictures of excellence.

Job Contribution	Career Success Skills	Relationships

3. Refresh them daily.

If you put your objectives and plans in a dusty file, they will not help you. It is the same with your pictures of excellence. Include your word pictures in your reinforcements. Think of them morning and evening. If they are of special importance or difficulty, think about them two or three additional times throughout the day. Try dedicating your time waiting on the phone to reviewing your pictures of excellence.

Remember the first time you were in love. Chances are you didn't have any trouble finding time to think about the object of your affection. Use the same persistence for refreshing the pictures you want to achieve. Let them stimulate your creativity and action.

Wrap-Up for Part 6

To increase the benefit you gain from this part, check (✔) the ideas that have the most value for you.

- ❑ I am motivated by what I am "missing."
- ❑ I can stimulate purposeful action by picturing what I want in wonderful detail.
- ❑ I can turn each important dream, objective, and target into a word picture because it is a handy way to access my mental picture.
- ❑ I find a picture of excellence for each priority area in my personal and professional life.
- ❑ Building teamwork is easier with a shared picture of excellence to pull the group in a unified direction.
- ❑ Building initiative and self-management is easier when I communicate a picture of excellence for our group's objective.

P A R T 7

Reinforcements that Work

"*No problem can stand the assault of sustained thinking.*"

—Voltaire

SUCCESS SECRET

Reinforce the best.

The Right Reinforcements for You

Matt glanced at the group around the conference table and explained, "The area where I need to improve? I don't even have to think about it. My problem is listening. When people talk to me, I'm practicing my response rather than hearing what they are saying. On Saturday, my wife told me again that she could barely get the words out of her mouth before I tossed her a solution. On Monday, a man at work told me that I didn't listen. I got hit with that twice in three days. My back was to the wall. I decided I had to change from playing a mouth to playing an ear."

In Matt's campaign to use his ears more than his mouth, his first draft of reinforcements sounded like this:

"I am going to listen better."

"Listening is not a waste of time."

"People think I am a good listener."

He then shaped them into more workable reinforcements:

"I score with listening."

"I enjoy listening and I learn a lot."

"I listen for facts and feelings."

Matt produced winning reinforcements because he:

- Picked the key arena he wanted to improve
- Tapped into the power of reinforcements that are present, positive, personal, playful, and challenging

Your Growing Edge

Reinforcements need to fit you. You will get the best results with the right reinforcements for your personality, your priorities, and your problems. So what are fast ways to make sure you have the right topics in your self-talk reinforcement system?

Pick the areas where you want to accomplish more and contribute more—your pictures of excellence, targets, and objectives. Put together a strong offense. Then pay attention to any barriers that stand in your way in those areas. These reinforcements give you a good defense.

When you use reinforcements that are written skillfully, they prompt you to take the action you want—consistently. So make sure your reinforcements work for you.

Self-Talk Traps and Safeguards

If you hear someone say, "I tried it once and it didn't work," flash the red warning light. The person was probably using defective self-talk statements. Defects and traps are common. Watch out for them.

The following chart reveals five big traps plus how you can steer clear of each one.

Traps		**Safeguards**
Fuzzy time frame	➜	Present
Negativity	➜	Positive
Focus on others	➜	Personal
Dull feeling	➜	Playful
Low horizon	➜	Challenging

The first three safeguards—present, positive, and personal—are the most important; the last two add zest and excitement. Let's look at examples that will help you make sure you have reinforcements that work for you.

Safeguard 1: Present

Reinforcements are best stated as a present belief, not as a hoped-for future attainment. They are designed to enhance behavior today. Using "will" delays the benefit.

Replace: I will Grab 15.

Use: *I Grab 15.*

Replace: We will get feedback from our customers on how well we are meeting requirements.

Use: *We get feedback from our customers on how well we are meeting requirements.*

The purpose of reinforcements is to get our present behavior to conform to our new beliefs. Our minds tend to put off implementing reinforcements that are stated in the future tense.

Practice

Rewrite these statements bringing them into the present.

1. I will do it now.

____

2. I am going to lose weight.

____

3. Someday I am going to get a job where I can contribute.

____

4. I am going to get these references organized.

____

5. I am going to start talking to people about opportunities in my organization.

____

Safeguard 2: Positive

Because our word pictures and self-talk have such pulling power, do not let them pull you backward. Move ahead with reinforcements that are positive. People who say to themselves, "I don't procrastinate," are looking at past performance and also at negative performance. It is like looking in the rearview mirror at where you have been, rather than looking at where you want to be.

Replace: I don't procrastinate.

Use: *I do it now.*

Replace: I am never over budget.

Use: *I am always on budget.*

Just as you do not drive while looking in the rearview mirror, do not train your mind by looking at where you do not want to be. Look instead at where you want to be.

Practice

Rewrite these statements and weave in the positive.

1. No more time spent hunting. No more lost items.

___

2. I'm not going to go to pieces.

___

3. I don't have defects in my work.

___

4. I don't have any difficult people at work.

___

5. I'm always running behind at work.

___

Safeguard 3: Personal

The best reinforcements reflect our role in achieving our own targets and objectives. The most useful focus is on changing ourselves, not others.

Replace: They don't appreciate me.

Use: *I ask for what I want.*

Replace: You'll never make it.

Use: *You can do it too.*

We are not responsible for what others do to us, how others treat us, or whether others appreciate us. We are responsible for ourselves, what we do to others, and how well we appreciate them and ourselves. This personal, self-responsibility focus must be reflected in the way our reinforcements are written.

Practice

Work through the following statements to make them personal.

1. They should know what I want.

____

2. I am just waiting until someone notices.

____

3. I shouldn't have to tell them.

____

4. My boss should motivate me.

____

5. You can't do it.

____

Check Your Rewrites

Are your rewrites close to these? Use these as ideas only. The sample statements can be improved in many different ways.

Present Examples:

"I do it now."

"I see myself weighing my goal weight."

"I am making a solid contribution in my job."

"I have well-organized references."

"I talk to people every day about opportunities in my organization."

Positive Examples:

"No temporary parking places. I put it in place or in use."

"I take care of my needs and wants in positive ways. I take purposeful action and I feel better."

"I produce work that is defect free, on time, every time."

"I am on time and frequently early. I get a kick out of getting things done in advance."

Personal Examples:

"I ask for what I want from people who can give it to me."

"I let people know what I have accomplished."

"I ask directly."

"I read my reinforcements daily. I put together pictures of excellence and processes to get there."

"You can do it too."

Safeguard 4: Playful

Each of us has more energy and commitment when life is fun. You will be more effective when you sprinkle playfulness into your reinforcements. For example:

Replace: I do not stop until I have finished a task.

Use: *I finish fully, and I feel great.*

Replace: I weigh my goal weight.

Use: *I love bouncing over to that scale, and it shows my goal weight.*

Replace: I see myself taking the stairs at work.

Use: *I enjoy seeing myself bounding up those stairs at work.*

Safeguard 5: Challenging

We are not inspired by just getting by. The plus side–doing well, achieving financial freedom, feeling good, or earning an award–is what motivates.

Replace: I just want to get through the day.

Use: *I turn problems into opportunities.*

Replace: I want to have enough money to pay the bills.

Use: *I do things every day to achieve financial freedom.*

Replace: I just hope my customers don't call about these problems.

Use: *I get the specifics so we can prevent problems.*

The most energizing reinforcements encourage productive action. They give you a mental pat on the back and a look in the right direction. They communicate, "You can do it! And the time to do it is now!"

It is difficult to completely remove old messages that do not work. Once you recognize them, though, outnumber them with a flood of constructive reinforcements–like "taping over" the old messages.

Fine-Tuning Your Mental Background Music

As you listen to what you say to yourself, think: "I am interested in honestly hearing the messages I repeat to myself. If I am saying things that drag me down, I want to recognize them. If I am saying things that direct and lift, I want to appreciate them." Turn up the volume. Listen closely to yourself. You may be surprised at what you learn.

Childhood Messages Are Still on the Job Today

As you tune into messages that are bouncing around your mind, be aware of when you learned the messages. Many of them you picked up as a child. Today these messages still have a powerful influence on who you are and what you do.

Much of the growth we want to experience involves replacing habits, patterns, and messages we learned in childhood. This is not an indictment of parents. Our parents did the best they could with what they had.

One goal of purposeful self-talk is to re-parent and re-coach ourselves into even more productive patterns and toward more meaningful goals, which we as self-responsible and self-directed adults consciously choose.

Tune In to the Messages You Learned in Childhood

Because the messages we say to ourselves have so much impact, they deserve some discovery time. To jump-start your thoughts, look over the following list. What messages did you learn about each of these topics? Jot down the first ideas that come to your mind. If nothing occurs to you about a particular topic, skip it and go on.

Being successful ______________________

Making a lot of money ______________________

Being famous ______________________

Getting what you want ______________________

Being happy ______________________

Your name ______________________

Your nicknames ______________________

Education ______________________

Pressure ______________________

Working ______________________

Hard work ______________________

Relaxing ______________________

Where you would end up ______________________

Who you would be like ______________________

Making decisions ______________________

Overcoming obstacles ______________________

Getting ahead ______________________

As Destructive as Sticks and Stones

As a child, you probably heard "Sticks and stones may break my bones, but names will never hurt me." The fact is that name-calling can and does hurt us all the time. Consider the following questions:

- Did anyone ever call you names as a child or adolescent? How do you feel about those names now as you recall them?
- More importantly, do you ever call yourself those names?

Peel Off Those Labels

Some people call themselves stupid, crazy, bad, failure, or ugly. For example, "I'm bad. I didn't do the report on time." That is a negative label. It drills into a person a sense of defeat and condemnation. This kind of label doesn't help anyone. A positive label works much better. Or the statement could be rewritten to make it constructive and motivating, such as "I did not do the report on time. I have solved problems like this before, and I am taking action to solve this one and to prevent it in the future." A rule of thumb for negative labels:

Change them to positive labels or change them to a description with encouragement to take purposeful action.

Reinforcements that Encourage

Many people did not hear the appreciation and encouragement they wanted and needed as a child. Such individuals often feel frustrated with others on the job. As adults, it is tempting for these people to expect others at work to give them what they missed when there were growing up..

But we can fill this gap ourselves. First, remember that our parents did the best they could with what they had. This clears away resentment. Second, include the missing reinforcements.

Excellent resources for these reinforcements and special coaching are the research and work of Robert M. Goulding, M.D., and Mary McClure Goulding, M.S.W. You will find solid ideas in their books *Redecision Therapy* and *Not To Worry*.

Replace: I can't ever win.
Use: *I am on my way!*

Replace: I am never good enough.
Use: *Of course I am a success!*

Replace: I don't feel important.
Use: *Of course I am important.*

Replace: I always feel like an outsider.
Use: *Make room for me.*

Replace: I never was a kid.
Use: *It's not too late for a happy childhood.*

Replace: There's something wrong with me.
Use: *I am all right the way I am.*

Reinforcements that encourage are powerful tools. Use the ones that work for you.

Wrap-Up for Part 7

To help you build habits of listening to your self-talk and rewriting messages that do not work into messages that do, check (✔) the concepts from this part that you found most helpful:

- ❑ I steer clear of five pitfalls: the fuzzy time frame, negativity, focus on others, dull feeling, and low horizon.
- ❑ I make sure my reinforcements are present, positive, personal, playful, and challenging.
- ❑ Purposeful action is my focus. The best reinforcements prompt me to take action in the right direction.

In the next part, you will get to know a woman who stepped out and overcame tremendous obstacles by consistently and persistently using pictures of excellence.

PART 8

Persistence, Pictures, and a Happy Ending

"*The future belongs to those who believe in the beauty of their dreams.*"

–Eleanor Roosevelt

SUCCESS SECRET

Persistence pays.

Keep on picturing what you want in wonderful detail.

Barbara's Success Story

Success stories widen our horizons and inspire us to keep moving toward our own dreams. Every once in a while a story does even more. It touches a deeper chord. It says in undeniable ways, "You can do it too!" Such is the story of Barbara.

Barbara's case study is so dramatic that it almost seems unbelievable. Yet, Barbara's story is true. The results she achieved are real. Barbara is someone who had every right to say, "I tried it once and it didn't work." But Barbara's story illustrates that the path to achievement is paved with persistence.

A Solid Foundation

You will understand Barbara's story better when you know that she had built a foundation. For six years she had attended weekly meetings in a 12-step program. In working the steps, she had developed the habit of mentally reinforcing helpful beliefs day by day. In addition, for four years, she had invested in family therapy for herself and her two children. Here are Barbara's own words as she spoke to the group in a follow-up seminar.

"My life reads like *The Perils of Pauline*!" Barbara said. A 30-something brunette with a penchant for self-deprecation, Barbara was desperate, depressed, and 70 pounds overweight. She made jokes at her own expense, such as "I go to the tent section to buy my dresses. And I always avoid bridges. Their load limit is 10 tons."

With surprising frankness, Barbara shared her story. Divorced after 17 years of marriage to a physically and mentally abusive alcoholic, Barbara was convinced she was a loser. Illness and misery stalked her constantly. When her husband discontinued child support, she and her two children moved in with her mother. "And that," she added, "was no day at the beach."

Four Packs of Cigarettes and Nine Bouts of Pneumonia

Barbara smoked four packs of cigarettes a day despite nine bouts with pneumonia and pleurisy. When doctors discovered signs of emphysema, she stopped smoking and her weight gain began. A routine exam revealed a tumor on her thyroid. Surgery confirmed it was malignant. Barbara underwent radiation treatment and gained more weight. Meanwhile, her father and a close friend died of lung cancer.

"I was miserable most of the time," she admitted. "I was convinced I was going to die. I figured cancer was everywhere. You feel as if your body has turned against you. You're only buying time."

She made out her will and even tagged Post-it notes to her possessions, with the names of those who were to inherit each item. Weeks passed and Barbara was surprised to find she was still alive, even though her doctors assured her the malignancy was being controlled and had not spread.

"I Can't Go Out Tonight. I Have Cancer."

Barbara returned to work in an administrative position and resumed her life. At about this time, she received a phone call from a man she had dated years before "Hi Barbara," he said. "I hear you're divorced now. I was wondering if you'd like to go out."

"Oh, no, I'm sorry," said Barbara. "I've gotten really fat and I don't date."

"It doesn't have to be a date. How about just going out for a drink?"

"I'm sorry, but I don't drink."

"Well, you say you're really fat, so you must eat. Would you like to go out for dinner?"

"No, I don't think so. I've been through a terrible trauma with my divorce and I'm not quite over it yet."

"Really? How long have you been divorced?"

"Three and a half years."

A few weeks later another man called and asked her out to a movie. "Oh, thank you," she said, "but I can't. I have cancer."

Dead silence.

Losing a Gymnast

"Those conversations show what my mental attitude was like," Barbara explained to the group. "Everything focused on my being sick. Every morning I'd wake up, hit the snooze alarm seven times, drag myself to the shower, and by the time I yanked my pantyhose on, I was so tired and out of breath I had to sit down and rest.

"I didn't walk anywhere. Even though my office was only two buildings away from the cafeteria, I drove to lunch every day. Every night after work, I put on my pajamas, took my dinner upstairs to my bed, and spent the evening eating and watching TV. I lived that way for years.

"Finally my doctor told me I had to lose 77 pounds. That was the year of the Olympics when media attention was focused on Mary Lou Retton. She weighed 78 pounds. I thought, "The doctor wants me to lose a small gymnast! How in the world can I do it?!"

Self-Fulfilling Prophecies

"About this time, I attended my first seminar. The trainer handed out packets of preprinted blue cards to everybody. Each of those cards contained a positive statement, such as:

I concentrate	I turn problems into opportunities	I picture what I want to accomplish in wonderful detail

"The trainer explained, 'If you put positive reinforcements in your mind, your behavior will gradually change to reflect what your mind believes to be true.'

"I was intrigued. Could it really be true that you are what you tell yourself you are? I realized that my self-talk was absolutely terrible! I was always telling myself, 'I'm tired. I don't feel good. I'm sick. I'm stupid. I can't win.' A whole string of self-sabotaging, self-fulfilling prophecies. Sure, I believed in positive thinking. I just figured it worked only for people who were already positive. After listening to the trainer, I thought I might actually be able to change and become a positive person myself.

"Next, the trainer handed out blank cards and told us to write down our wishes or desires–and to state them as positive affirmations. She said, 'If you want to lose weight, write down what you want to weigh. For example, 'I am a 120-pound woman. I picture myself at my goal weight.'

"Well, that got my attention!

"But I was skeptical too. Easy for her to say this self-talk works. She's cute, thin, and smart. She travels all around the world and she's financially independent. She probably has a husband who's thin, cute, and smart too!"

Doing It Anyway

But Barbara dutifully wrote out her reinforcements–statements that expressed a belief in the future possibilities to conquer present realities. "I was 70 pounds overweight when I wrote out the card that said, 'I am a 120-pound woman.' I was snacking on spaghetti and garlic bread when I wrote, 'I love raw vegetables. If I am tempted to graze, I reach for the raw veggies.' I was out of breath after getting dressed in the morning when I wrote, 'I walk a mile a day.' Those reinforcements contrasted so wildly with the way I really lived that I could hardly bring myself to read the cards."

Barbara took the cards home despite her skepticism. "I showed my mother," she said. "Actually I would have liked to have brought her a stack too!" Barbara put the cards on her nightstand, intending to start building good self-talk habits into her life. Instead, the cards collected dust for the next three months.

"One Saturday morning on my way to work, I stopped at Bagels and Doughnuts and bought a dozen doughnuts. I planned to have a few doughnuts at work, then take the rest home. By three in the afternoon, that doughnut box was completely empty. Of the two other people who were there, only one had eaten a doughnut. I realized I had eaten all the rest myself! That evening I went out to dinner with a friend. I had a big meal at Howard Johnson's and topped it off with a maple-walnut sundae. I went home feeling absolutely miserable."

A Turning Point

"That was a turning point in my thinking. I felt like Scarlet in *Gone with the Wind* when she raised her arm skyward and swore that she would never be poor again. In my bedroom that night, I raised my arm upward and I swore, 'I have had it! I swear, as God is in heaven, I will never be fat again!'

"That night," she recalled, "I was lying in bed when I noticed those cards from the seminar. I picked them up in desperation. The doctor had ordered me to lose 77 pounds, but nothing worked. I figured I had nothing to lose–or should I say everything to lose–so I decided to read those cards.

"The next day I pulled on my sweat suit and drove to the track in a park near home. Somehow I made it around the track even though I had to sit and rest on the bench at each quarter-mile.

"I kept on reading my cards faithfully every day, morning and evening, for one month. And at the end of 30 days, exactly nothing happened.

"My seminar leader had guaranteed that I would get results if I would read the cards for 60 days. So I kept on reading every morning and evening."

An Amazing Discovery

"After five weeks, I found them so powerful," Barbara said, "I knew I would have to make changes in my life or stop reading the cards. My mind wanted to do what the cards said I was doing. Day after day, I kept reading my cards and picturing myself at my goal weight. I pictured my hand reaching into the refrigerator and picking up a handful of carrot sticks rather than the cold spaghetti. I kept picturing myself walking around the track. By this time, I was walking four miles every evening instead of watching TV. After seven weeks, I made an amazing discovery–the pounds were actually coming off!"

One Saturday, excited about her weight loss, Barbara threw her old clothes out a second-story window in their home. Her daughter was in the front yard and saw the clothes flying out the window. She cheered her mother, saying, "It's raining fat clothes!"

I Love My Life!

Two years later, Barbara is trim and attractive on the outside, full of poise, warmth, and self-confidence on the inside. Her cancer is in remission and she feels good. Now she exclaims, "I love my life! I'm at my goal weight and I have a whole new life. The changes in my body are the most obvious thing that's happened to me. But even more important is the change in my attitude about myself. That has affected not only my weight, but my work as well.

"I always thought I was an excellent administrator. I did everything I was supposed to do. But I didn't think my boss liked me all that much. I wasn't happy in my job.

"With my new self-confidence, I had an honest talk with my boss and learned he had requested me for the job because he liked my work. I was amazed. I thought he preferred someone else. How senseless to have gone all those months thinking he didn't want me!

"Since then, things have gone better in all areas of my life. My boss has given me more responsibility and extra projects. I've received $2,000 in accomplishment awards in the last six months."

Feeling Good About Yourself

"I've learned that when you feel good about yourself, it affects every area of your life. I don't tell mean jokes about myself anymore. Now they're on the positive side, such as 'When I'm a millionaire, I'll buy the biggest house in town.' Your mind registers as fact what you verbalize. That's why I'm still doing my cards every day. Here are some of them:

I see myself—from the inside out—at my goal weight.

I am happy.

I love my job.

I have a wonderful working relationship with my boss.

I am financially independent.

I enjoy my co-workers.

I exercise daily.

I'm a worthwhile person with great ideas.

I forgive my ex-husband.

I wear makeup and fix my hair every day.

I always eat healthy foods.

I know I can, I know I can, I know I can.

"But here's one of my best cards," Barbara declared. "I wrote it last year."

I have a wonderful, exciting social life with a kind, gentle, affectionate man.

If you ask Barbara if reinforcements work, she gives you a knowing smile. "You tell me," she replies. "I got married two weeks ago. You guessed it. To a kind, gentle, affectionate man."

Pictures and Supporting Processes

If you had a chance to talk with Barbara in person, what would you say to her?

____

____

Which success principles in Barbara's story do you see? (For example, "Keep using a good process for 60 days even if you don't see the results immediately.")

____

____

____

Barbara pictured herself accomplishing her objectives, her pictures of excellence, such as "I see myself at my goal weight wearing a size-6 red dress."

She also pictured herself using the practical, supporting processes that would help her reach her goal, including:

> *"I see my hand reaching into the refrigerator and picking up a handful of raw vegetables."*
>
> *"I see myself on Saturday morning preparing a big container of raw veggies to have as snacks for the week."*
>
> *"I see myself walking around the track four miles a day."*

What is another example of a picture and supporting process someone like Barbara might use?

Word picture: ____

____

Supporting process: ____

____

Designing Your Success Story

When you accomplish your dreams as Barbara did, specifically what will you be seeing? In other words, describe one of your pictures of excellence.

What are some supporting processes you can put into your reinforcements to help you accomplish your picture?

Some reinforcements Barbara wrote were uncomfortable for her. For example, she wrote, "I see myself at my goal weight wearing a size-6 red dress. I am a 120-pound woman." But she was thinking that such reinforcements contrasted so wildly with the way she really lived that she could hardly bring herself to read those cards.

What are the advantages to you of writing a word picture that stretches you beyond your comfort level?

Success stories always embody stretching and improving. And success stories add to your energy and persistence in pursuing your own happy endings.

Wrap-Up for Part 8

To help you build your pattern of persistence, check (✔) the ideas from this part that have the most value for you:

- ❑ When I fill my mind with positive reinforcements, my behavior will gradually change to reflect what my mind believes to be true.
- ❑ I write and read my reinforcements even if I am not comfortable with what they say because I know they represent self-fulfilling prophecies.
- ❑ I verbalize only the beliefs that will draw me forward rather than make mean jokes about my defects.
- ❑ I not only imagine pictures of excellence; I also imagine practical, supporting processes that will help me reach my targets.
- ❑ I am a person of persistence because I know that persistence is the key to making the improvements I want.

In the next part, you will explore how you can enjoy this same powerful process in just seven days.

PART 9

The Seven-Day Quick Start

"*It doesn't matter when you start as long as you start now.*"

–W. Edwards Deming

SUCCESS SECRET

Do it anyway.

It is better to improve along the way than it is to perfect and delay.

Seven-Day Quick Start–Shortcut to Success

Here is how a group of seminar participants, both men and women, described their experiments with the Seven-Day Quick Start:

"It felt good even the first time."

"I was surprised that something so simple works so well."

"I did it in my car."

"I did it in bed."

"I did it faithfully for 39 days and nothing happened. Then on the 40th day ...."

"I had only 45 seconds of them and even that made a difference."

"You guys, this is hot. Do it."

You can enjoy these same results. The Quick-Start experiment takes only two minutes, twice a day. And you can do it anywhere. The Seven-Day Quick Start:

- Helps you to experience, not just hear, how easy it is to benefit from purposeful self-talk (reinforcements)
- Is simple, quick, and powerful

You simply read a short collection of self-talk reinforcements. These statements have been researched and proven. Over the past decade they have been used successfully by hundreds of seminar participants. They work.

Two Minutes Morning and Evening

Consider this exercise a gift to yourself. As you start, keep your collection of self-talk statements to less than two minutes. If you select more than two minutes of reinforcements, it is too tempting to push them aside.

Invest these two minutes in yourself the first thing in the morning and the last thing at night. Many people are the most receptive just before fully waking and before going to sleep. But you can read your reinforcements during the day at any two times and still get good results. Read the reinforcements aloud for maximum benefit. The more of your senses you involve in your learning, the more value you will receive.

Each time you read your reinforcements, reward yourself with a star or check mark on your daily calendar. You may be surprised how a simple reward system motivates. In some ways, most of us are children at heart, enjoying the fun of earning stars. Use any simple reward system that works for you.

Success Tips

The Place

The Seven-Day Quick Start works best when you anchor this new habit to a place or an activity you already do each day. Some people read their reinforcements in bed upon awaking and again before going to sleep. Others read them after brushing their teeth, morning and evening. Some people read while riding in the car pool to and from work. Still others review their reinforcements with a cup of coffee after breakfast and dinner. Your creativity will lead you to the way to link your reinforcements to your daily patterns.

Doing It Anyway

Because the reinforcements that follow take only two minutes to read, you can read them all, or you can pick the ones that especially apply to you.

Some people feel guilty the first time they read these reinforcements. They know the ideas already, and they also know they have not been fully implementing them. If you are one of those people, forgive yourself and keep moving forward. Some people feel guilty if they miss a time. If you do, you can make it up the next day. You will soon replace any guilt with satisfaction and accomplishment.

You may want to put your reinforcements on three-by-five-inch cards. Writing one idea to a card makes the reinforcements easy to update. If you do not have cards handy, you can read the list out of this book. Whatever you do, now is a great time to do it.

Making It Easy for Yourself

The second set of reinforcements, marked with a star (★), is specially designed to keep your reinforcement system going. They put gas in the tank. You will get better, more consistent results when you include them each time you read your reinforcements.

Investing in Yourself for Seven More Days

After the first seven days, invest in yourself again. The first exhilarating taste makes it easier for you to do it for another week. As you go along, ideas for refining your reinforcements will occur to you. Add them. Take out the ones you no longer want. Make this an ongoing process of self-talk and self-coaching that will enable you to enjoy more satisfaction and add more value.

The 60-Day Guarantee

People who are feeling stress often say that 60 days is too long a commitment, so planning for seven days at a time works well. The most power and best results come from using your reinforcements for 60 days. Among the hundreds of seminar attendees who used the reinforcements, those who invested two minutes, morning and evening, for 60 days experienced a 95% success rate. They gained the improvements they wanted.

The key: The Right Reinforcements plus Consistency

2 + 2 x 60 = Less Stress, More Motivation, and Better Results

Dru Scott Quick-Start Set of Reinforcements

To build motivation:

- ➤ I always have choices.
- ➤ There is always something I can do.
- ➤ I turn problems into opportunities, so I am always in a good mood.
- ➤ I picture what I want in snapshot detail, because pictures add to my drive and my discipline.
- ➤ I focus and I finish.
- ➤ I get closure.

To keep myself up, out, and on the right road:

- ★ I read my reinforcements aloud to myself. This is a great way to cut stress, add energy, and get the right things done.
- ★ I give myself an extra lift, because I read my reinforcements in the morning and evening.
- ★ It's fun to put together the word pictures that motivate me.
- ★ I put together both pictures of excellence and processes to get there.
- ★ I get a kick out of marking a star on my calendar each time I read my reinforcements.

If I feel stress, I picture a baseball diamond like this:

- At first base, I relax and breathe deeply for a few moments.
- At second base, I accept my feelings and the realities of my current situation.
- At third base, I picture how I want the situation to be.
- At home plate, I do something. I take action–some step–toward my picture, a solution, or mastery.
- When I take an action step toward my picture, a solution, or mastery, I feel relief. I feel energy. And I feel light.
- I remember the baseball diamond with RAPiD: R for relax; A for accept; P for picture; and D for do something.

To keep my energy level high:

- I pay attention to my feelings. I respect my feelings. I name my feelings.
- I help people get what they want.
- My customers are happy to hear from me because I help them get what they want.
- I Grab 15. It's incredible how much I can accomplish in 15 minutes a day.
- I picture this sign by my telephone: "No temporary parking places." I put things in place or in use.

To build teamwork and relationships:

- If I have a difficult person in my life, I pull out the sign with the seven power words: "I fix my part of the problem."
- Blaming strips people of their power, so I solve problems without blaming.
- I forgive and I feel free.
- I fix the process and not the person.
- I prevent problems.
- I ask for what I want.
- I help put together win-win solutions.

To enjoy today:

- This is a great day.
- My quiet time is the high point of my day.
- I have a big smile as I exercise. After only 30 minutes I feel so much more energy.
- I never have a dull moment because I am always working to cross off items on my weekly target sheet.
- I give myself a head start because I do the toughest top priority first.
- I do what counts.
- I do it anyway.
- I do it now!

Wrap-Up for Part 9

As a first step toward building the Quick-Start Reinforcement process into your life, check (✔) the ideas that are the most important to you:

- ❑ I know it is better to start now and improve along the way than to delay and wait for the perfect time.
- ❑ Even if I do not have the perfect set of reinforcements to use for my purposeful self-talk, I can start now.
- ❑ I have a starter set of reinforcements that have been researched and proven useful by hundreds of people.
- ❑ I can read my reinforcements from the Seven-Day Quick-Start list or I can put each idea on a card and read them individually.
- ❑ I read my reinforcements in the morning and evening.
- ❑ To reward myself, I mark a star or check on my daily calendar.

Enjoy Continuous Improvement

Stress That Motivates
Self-Talk Secrets for Success

It forms how you feel.
It directs what you do.
It shapes what you earn.

Yet it:
Costs only pennies,
Takes only minutes.

And it
Is one of those things in life
That is totally within your control.

It is
What you say to yourself.
It is particularly
What you say to yourself over and over,
Your mental background music.

So fill your mind with the music that
Encourages you,
Directs you
and
Inspires you.

Invest two minutes each morning and evening in purposeful self-talk–your reinforcements.

Acknowledgments

The participants in my seminars and speeches–for all they have taught me.

Al Beller, my first manager in a career job–for telling me years ago, "Dru, rather than concentrating on things you can't change, accept them. Work on things you can change; and by all means, change what you say to yourself."

Bert Decker, my husband–for being such an inspiration to me; and for my family: Allison, Sam, and Ben–for calling on me to grow and be my best.

DuPont–for funding the research and seminars behind much of this book. What a privilege to work with an organization so committed to people and continuous improvement.

Barbara Latta–for her inspiring story.

Mike Crisp–for being such a visionary in publishing.

Frank Nuessle, Crisp Publications–for dreaming up title #89–Stress That Motivates: Self-Talk Secrets for Success. As soon as he said it, we all agreed, "Yes, this is it!"

Kathleen Barcos–for her grace in juggling all the pieces that fall into the hands of an executive editor.

Carol Gift Page and Jim Denney–for being such great trainers on putting life into writing.

For the people who have added so much to me and this book: Lenora Borecek; Robert Bronzan, Ph.D.; Mary Butler; Lowell Dicke; Peter F. Drucker; Stephen DeVeber; Bill Kirkey; Claire Lee; Lenora Leffert; Dave English; Jane Janson; Stephen Karpman, M.D.; Elizabeth Paeth Lasker, M.D.; Kris Poggioli; Jennifer Tan; and Mahlia Riebeling.

Debbie Woodbury–for her persistence and leadership as the Executive Editor for the Revised Edition of *Stress That Motivates*.

Additional Reading

Braham, Barbara and Chris Wahl. *Be Your Own Coach.* Menlo Park, CA: Crisp Publications, 2000.

Chapman, Elwood N. and Wil McKnight. *Attitude: Your Most Priceless Possession.* Menlo Park, CA: Crisp Publications, 2001.

Emery, Gary, Ph.D., and Campbell, James, M.D. *Rapid Relief from Emotional Distress: A New, Clinically Proven Method for Getting Over Depression and Other Emotional Problems Without Prolonged or Expensive Therapy.* NY: Ballantine Books, A Fawcett Columbine Book, 1986.

Gallwey, W. Timothy. *The Inner Game of Work.* NY: Random House, 2000.

Goulding, Robert L., M.D. and Goulding, Mary McClure. *Changing Lives Through Redecision Therapy.* NY: Brunner/Mazel Publishers, 1979.

Goulding, Robert L., M.D. and Goulding, Mary McClure. *Not to Worry! How to Free Yourself from Unnecessary Anxiety and Channel Your Worries into Positive Action.* NY: William Morrow Silver Arrow Books, 1989.

Kindler, Herb and Marilyn Ginsburg. *Measure and Manage Stress.* Menlo Park, CA: Crisp Publications, 1994.

LaHaye, Tim. *How to Win Over Depression.* Grand Rapids, MI: Zondervan Publishing House, 1996.

Peck, M. Scott, M.D. *The Road Less Traveled: A New Psychology of Love, Traditional Values and Spiritual Growth.* NY: Simon & Schuster, 1978.

Potter, Beverly A., Ph.D. *Preventing Job Burnout: Transforming Work Pressures Into Productivity.* Menlo Park, CA: Crisp Publications, 1987.

Raber, Merrill F. and George Dyck. *Managing Stress for Mental Fitness.* Menlo Park, CA: Crisp Publications, 1993.

NOTES

NOTES